ESCAPE
THE
MIDDLE

ESCAPE THE MIDDLE

SWITCH ON
YOUR
**MILLIONAIRE
MINDSET**
AND BUILD
WEALTH
THAT
OUTLIVES
YOU

**TODD
POLKE**

WILEY

First published 2025 by John Wiley & Sons Australia, Ltd

© John Wiley & Sons Ltd, Australia 2025

The right of Todd Polke to be identified as the author of *Escape the Middle* has been asserted in accordance with law.

ISBN: 978-1-394-30399-1

A catalogue record for this book is available from the National Library of Australia

Registered Office
John Wiley & Sons Australia, Ltd. Level 4, 600 Bourke Street, Melbourne, VIC 3000, Australia

For details of our global editorial offices, customer services, and more information about Wiley products visit us at www.wiley.com.

Wiley also publishes its books in a variety of electronic formats and by print-on-demand. Some content that appears in standard print versions of this book may not be available in other formats.

Cover and internal page images: © Gebbi Mur/Getty Images, © i_fleur/Shutterstock
Cover design by Wiley

Set in 10.5/16pt and Plantin Std by Straive, Chennai, India

SKY8C78EB86-04B3-4A09-8832-0DADC16E2B6C_030725

CONTENTS

ABOUT THE AUTHOR

Todd Polke is an investor, entrepreneur and international educator with over two decades of experience in wealth creation and investing. Having guided thousands of investors to build high-performing portfolios and facilitated over $4 billion in global investment opportunities, Todd is dedicated to empowering individuals to achieve financial freedom and create lasting legacies for themselves and their families.

As the founder of Portfolio Wealth, Todd leads an investment education company that helps everyday investors take control of their financial lives, develop high-performance portfolios and unlock their full financial potential. Known for his approachable style and ability to simplify complex financial concepts, Todd has earned a reputation as a trusted mentor for those seeking to improve their financial futures.

Todd's philosophy centres on building 'wealth with purpose,' aligning financial success with personal and planetary impact. He is deeply committed to supporting ventures that drive positive change, using his expertise to lead funding for companies that contribute to a better world.

A devoted husband, father of two and philanthropist, Todd believes wealth is not just about financial freedom—it's about creating a meaningful life, leaving a legacy and making a difference. Through his proven systems and personalised strategies, Todd continues to inspire others to pursue their passions and build a brighter future.

ACKNOWLEDGEMENTS

To my dearest wife, Nerissa, my greatest gift, my everything. My devotion to you is eternal.

To my daughter, Annabelle (aka Mouse). Watching you grow into the amazing young woman you are today fills me with pride.

To my son, Atlas (aka Squiggs). Your mischievous smile and laugh light up my world. Seeing your determination shine through before you've even turned one—watch out, world!

To my teacher and mentors, for seeing parts of me that I was yet to see. I would not be who I am today without you.

Finally, to the many thousands of you who have put your trust in me to be your guide in the worlds of money and life, from the bottom of my heart, thank you.

PREFACE

Financial slavery is a relentless cycle of trading time for money, grinding hard but getting nowhere. It's the treadmill we've all been conditioned to accept, the way of the 'middle'. And if you're reading this, I'm betting you're fed up with it.

This model of living broke me at a young age and left me questioning why we were never shown an alternative in the traditional education system. Then I found a better path.

I believe freedom is your birthright and it's time you took it back! For more than two decades I've helped countless investors break free, empowering them to take control of their finances, build the wealth they deserve and live life to the fullest.

Imagine a life where money is no longer a source of stress but is rather a tool to help you fully experience life. How different would it feel to have more time, freedom and choices to pursue what you love, follow your passions, and give back to your family and the world?

You picked up this book because you're searching for a new path— a life that isn't limited by your income or the hours you work. And it's absolutely within your reach. The wealthy don't succeed by chance; they follow a different set of rules for life and money, and anyone can learn them.

But learning wealth-building strategies alone is only half the game. Reaching new levels of success requires a new level of thinking.

This book provides both: the mindset and the money-making strategies to guide you, step by step, out of the middle and into a life where building wealth and freedom becomes as natural as paying a bill.

The journey out of the 'middle'

You're about to uncover a proven investment roadmap—a carefully curated selection of tools, systems and strategies that have been rigorously road-tested and are grounded in real-world experience.

This journey goes beyond managing money; it's about reclaiming your life. By mastering the money game as the wealthy do, you'll break free from financial stress and open doors to the lifestyle you deserve.

You'll define your *financial freedom figure*. This is your escape plan number—a clear, empowering target that represents more than just money. It's your pathway to living life on your own terms, without the burden of bills or unexpected expenses holding you back.

Achieving new results demands a new mindset. We'll activate your *millionaire mode*, uncovering the hidden saboteurs from years of poor financial conditioning and unlocking opportunities you've never imagined.

You'll take charge as the CEO of your own finances, and as you gain control your anxiety will give way to clarity and purpose.

In just one hour a week, I'll teach you a simple, powerful habit to put your finances on autopilot, ensuring every dollar has a clear plan and purpose.

The wealth-building system I've perfected over twenty-plus years will be yours. We'll create a plan to make your money work for you, breaking the paycheque-to-paycheque cycle. Whether you're new to investing or have limited capital, I'll guide you, step by step, to start building wealth from where you are now.

You'll discover the *three strategies every successful investor needs* to grow and scale their wealth, strategies that the rich have been using for generations to secure their future.

Next, we'll build a financial fortress to protect you, your family and your portfolio as you grow your wealth. It's about ensuring you're secure, no matter what life brings, so you can confidently keep moving forward.

Finally, we'll dive into the *four levels of legacy*, teaching you how to create a portfolio that serves you now but also outlives you, ensuring your impact lasts for generations. It's about more than just money; it's about building a life of freedom and purpose and a lasting legacy. And so much more. This is the financial education we all should have been taught in school.

Getting the most out of this book

Each concept we'll cover builds on the last, so it's best to read this book sequentially, rather than skipping around. These strategies have already guided countless investors to financial freedom, and they can do the same for you. But, like anything, these tools only work if you use them. Take action, implement and watch your results transform your life. This system works—if you work the system.

I often remind my students, 'Learn one thing, do one thing.' Implementation is key. Each chapter gives you the chance to act and is designed to shift your financial trajectory towards freedom.

These strategies work. I've applied them in my own life and helped thousands do the same. But it requires your time, focus and commitment—there are no silver bullets. Many spend years getting into their current financial situation, yet they hope to magically transform it overnight. It doesn't happen like that. While your trajectory can shift quickly, real results come through sustained focus.

But isn't your freedom worth it? Isn't having more time, more choice and the opportunity to fully experience life worth the effort?

Before we begin this journey I want you to know how much respect I have for you, the investor. You're choosing not to follow the crowd, and that takes courage, guts, commitment and a vision of living life on your own terms rather than blindly following what you've been taught.

So I honour you, and as you turn this page and start reading, know that you're not alone. Many other financial renegades, just like you, are walking this path alongside you.

PART I

ESCAPE THE MIDDLE

CHAPTER 1

WELCOME TO THE MIDDLE

You may know this place…It's where most people tend to hang out in life. You may have arrived here just by following along with what everyone around you does, playing by the same set of rules and doing practically the same thing each and every day.

It can feel safe and certain in this place called the middle; after all, the path is well trodden. Yet the middle is also a place of unrealised potential.

You may find yourself feeling 'middle happy'. Things aren't that great, but they're also not bad enough for you to feel the need to change course.

Maybe you feel trapped at a 'middle income' level, exhausted, going round and round on the 'work to pay the bills' financial slavery hamster wheel. You know deep down there must be more to life than you can find in this space. But you have all these excuses and justifications for why it's too late or now is not the right time, or fanciful dreams around how you will do it one day when... (insert your excuse here).

Let's explore the pathway of the middle.

How did you get here?

Is this what you dreamed about when you were younger? Did you think to yourself, 'YES! The middle is the place for me!' Think back to when you were young... What did you then imagine was possible for you? Was there a limit to your potential? What did you dream life was all about?

Now think honestly about your current life circumstances. Look around you and consider for a moment, are you where you want to be in life? Did you hope to be further along in some way? More stable financially, having further progressed in your career? Experiencing more happiness and joy or a fulfilling relationship?

Ask yourself, how did you get here?

Middle comfort

Somewhere along the way on this journey called life we start to build walls around us to stay safe. These walls are based on all the experiences we have had in life, and our conclusions about what is safe and what is unsafe. These beliefs tend to confine us to a 'safe room' within walls we ourselves have built.

Imagine yourself in this space. By the time you read this you may have spent most of your life right here inside these walls. You know how high they are and how much room you have to move around within them. You know which rooms feel good and which feel less so.

As you stand there just noticing, your eyes settle on the first wall right in front of you. The wall is adorned with intertwined hearts; they seem quite beautiful. You notice there's a word etched on the wall, right in the centre. You look closer to make out what it says and you read the word 'relationships'.

Your *relationship wall* signifies all the ways in which you hold yourself back in your relationships. Behind this wall you stick to what is a safe level of connection for you. You may block yourself from fully committing or expressing your true feelings because past experiences have left scars, and the fear of getting hurt again is overwhelming.

You settle for a middle level of intimacy or connection.

Turning to your right, your gaze settles on the next wall and again you notice markings, including currency symbols and pictures of things you relate to money and wealth.

Your *money wall* represents the fears you hold about money, debt and investing. Behind this wall, you stick to what you know: your spending habits, your savings account and perhaps even some safe investments. You avoid financial risks because the thought of losing money is daunting. You may dream of investing in a new venture or starting a business or creating financial freedom, but the fear of failure keeps you behind the safety of this wall. Here, your financial life tends to stay more or less on the same trajectory. For better or worse, it is fairly predictable, but you may be missing out on opportunities to grow your wealth and achieve the financial freedom you deeply desire.

Another wall represents your day job. Your *work wall* constitutes the professional comfort zone you've built for yourself. Behind this wall you follow a routine, sticking to tasks and roles you've become accustomed to over time. You may be driven only by job security, afraid to go after what you truly want in life because you feel chained to a regular paycheque.

But are you truly happy in the place where you spend the biggest share of your time? Are you earning what you are worth, given how many hours you sacrifice here?

This wall may provide you with security, but it does so at the cost of confining you to a career path that may not allow you to realise your full potential.

You turn towards the final wall, emblazoned with the Yin-Yang symbol. This is your *health wall*. It reveals all your physical, mental, and emotional habits and routines. Do you push yourself to burnout, sacrificing too much of your life in pursuit of greater financial success? Or are you coasting, living far below your potential?

Have you caused yourself anxiety, stress and overwhelm, but avoided supportive practices such as meditation? Have you neglected your physical health by consuming junk food and skipping exercise?

This wall is often built on excuses:

- I'm too stressed.
- I don't know how.
- I'm too tired.

And, of course, everyone's favourite: I don't have time.

As a result, you can be left with a 'middling' level of energy, feeling dissatisfied about your body, with a mediocre level of clarity, achieving only a fraction of your health potential and watching this mediocrity affect other areas of your life.

You may be totally comfortable inside the walls you have built around you, because you feel like you can predict what is going to happen next and you have a semblance of control, so you feel safe. But these walls have become a prison, crushing your potential and greatest joy in life?

One of these walls may feel more relevant to you than another, but the truth is each of them has the potential to hold you back in the other areas.

Take your finances and wealth building. A mid-level health wall may mean you don't have the energy and confidence to go after your dreams and ambitions to grow your income and raise your value in the market.

A mid-level relationship wall may mean you lack the connection, trust and understanding you desire with your partner. Fights around money will emerge if your money lenses (more on this later) clash in an already charged area of life, and getting on the same page can be a real challenge.

A mid-level work wall may trap you with the promise of a steady paycheque, sacrificing your potential, day after day leaving you feeling unfulfilled and earning only a fraction of what you're worth.

Most people I meet want more out of life than they are currently experiencing: more happiness, experiences, joy, meaning, money and choices. But the biggest risk of all in life holds them back: they are trapped by fear.

It's not your fault

It might feel like I'm laying the blame squarely on your shoulders for where you are in life and how you're feeling, good or bad. I'm not, but I am a big believer in taking total and unequivocal responsibility for your own actions and results.

The truth is that most people have been trained to live within the confines of their walls and 'the middle' their entire life.

Family and friends

When you were young you felt like everything was possible. If someone asked you what you were going to be when you grew up, the sky was the limit!

Then, bit by bit, your dreams and imagination were tempered by experience. Was it your parents or caregivers who told you to 'get your head out of the clouds', 'be realistic', 'grow up', 'be responsible' and 'no, you can't have [or be] that'? Or perhaps you simply modelled your behaviour on their example.

But slowly you began to form a belief—conscious or unconscious—that maybe all those things you once thought possible were beyond your reach.

Education

The education system teaches us to colour within the lines, dress in a specific way, stand in a straight line, act in uniform ways and do what we are told. Every student is taught and graded in the same way, following the same standard curriculum, despite each of us being different. Hang on...what if we don't learn in that format? What if our natural skill sets lie in other areas, and we deliver best results in different formats?

We're programmed to believe in uniformity. We're rewarded for adhering to established rules and discouraged from thinking outside the box. As impressionable youths, we prioritise acceptance over exploring our unique genius and forging our own paths.

Society

You graduate and step into responsible adulthood—which you already know entails being a reliable, hard worker—and you fall into the 'work to pay the bills' financial slavery system. The rules are established and the entire pathway of your life is laid out before you, because that's what everyone else does so it must be right.

We do what we've been taught to believe is right and become just another functioning cog in an economic wheel of the middle of society. Middle-level happiness. Middle-level satisfaction. You don't have to think too much; you just have to follow along.

Raising your zero line

Most readers (and that includes you) have picked up this book for one of two reasons. Perhaps you have reached a point in your life, much as I did when I was younger, when you're feeling disillusioned. You're thinking, *Is this all there is? Surely there's a better way?* And you're actively looking for solutions to get out of 'the middle'.

Alternatively, things have become too painful for you to stay where you are in life. Your level of dissatisfaction has convinced you of the need for change, that staying where you are is no longer an option.

Both of these conditions tell me you want more out of life than the middle tends to offer. You want more choices, freedom and meaning.

So what is it going to take?

You've been operating at a certain frequency in your life to date, but that frequency is not going to get you to where you want to go. It's time to level up. It's time to 'raise your zero line' (see figure 1.1, overleaf).

Your zero line is the minimum standard to which you've been holding yourself to date. Think of it as your internal thermostat. Drop below your zero line and your thermostat kicks in and heats up your urgency and actions until you regain your zero. When you begin to ease off on the gas, the urgency fades, complacency settles in again and it's back to business as usual.

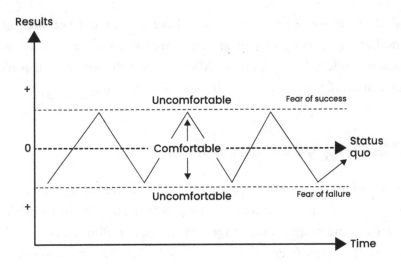

Figure 1.1: your zero line

Perhaps you didn't take the pedal off the gas and, heaven forbid, you rose above your zero line and started to exceed your previous results. What could possibly be wrong with that? It might sound like exactly what your thinking mind wants. But many people are just as uncomfortable with success as they are with failure. So the thermostat kicks in to cool things down. *It's too hot in here. Let's cool this baby down—right back to where we have always done things, because at least we know what to expect here and we feel comfortable.*

The Greek poet Archilochus famously said, 'We don't rise to the level of our expectations. We fall to the level of our training.' I'll swap out the word 'training' for 'standards', meaning our ways of thinking, deciding and acting consistently over a period of time to generate a particular result.

Raising your zero line means raising your consistent way of thinking, deciding and acting and committing to a new standard, which will generate a new result. Over time this becomes a part of who you are. It's no longer an effort; it's just your new way of being and then — the next level!

You know your zero line has changed. It doesn't mean you might not fall below it from time to time, and in fact you're probably guaranteed to do that. Accept this and decide now, ahead of time, how to respond when you do. Now you are no longer in a reactive state; rather, you are intentional and purposeful.

So ask yourself, *What has been the zero line I have been operating at to date?* Then ask, *What's the new zero line I want to commit to operating at?*

What about the zero line for your finances, for what you earn, for how much money you have in the bank, for your investments and how many income streams you have coming in?

Get back into your way of thinking when you were younger, when everything seemed possible. Did you know when you were younger that you were meant for more than what you might be living in your life right now?

This isn't to say that taking care of your finances and building wealth is going to solve all of your challenges in life. It won't. What it does, though, is it gives you back your life. It means no longer spending your time on the treadmill of life exchanging time for money on the never-ending work to pay the bills merry-go-round.

Financial security gives you choices for how you want to live and experience life. It gives you opportunities you could never access before because you lacked the resources. It allows you to take care of yourself and your family in every way that is meaningful to you.

It gives you the safety and certainty to go after something bigger in life, knowing your home base is covered.

It allows you to say *no* when you need to, and to be self-reliant. It gives you control over your and your family's future, so no matter what comes your way in life, you can handle it.

Money means choices.

I know all this, and even making the decision to change, sounds easy. But you can do that right now in this moment and never look back. Following through can be tougher. It takes *courage*.

It means challenging old belief systems, many of which are firmly entrenched and reinforced over decades.

It may mean intentionally choosing to spend more time with certain people and less time with others.

It means embracing change, including new habits and ways of thinking and doing.

It means following the road less travelled.

The good news is that just as there was a well-worn pathway that led you to the middle, there's another pathway that will help you escape it. It is a path to a different quality of life. A life where you realise your full potential.

It's a pathway to greater meaning, greater wealth, greater choices, greater giving, greater thinking. And it's available to you if you make one simple decision. You must decide to escape the middle once and for all and go after your potential.

So are you ready?

Let's go.

Power points

- The middle is the place of unrealised potential.

- There are four mental walls people tend to erect unconsciously to keep themselves safe:

  1. The **relationship wall** represents the ways you hold yourself back in your relationships.

  2. The **money wall** reflects the fears you have about money, debt and investing.

  3. The **work wall** constitutes the professional comfort zone you've built for yourself.

  4. The **health wall** reveals your physical, mental, and emotional habits and routines.

- Success in life is interconnected: your health, wealth, relationships and career influence one another. The quality of each can either accelerate or limit your progress.

- You've been conditioned to live within your mental walls by influences like family, friends, education and societal expectations. Whether or not you stay there is up to you.

- To break free from past conditioning you must raise your **zero line**.

- Your zero line, like an internal thermostat, is the minimum standard you've been holding yourself to. When you dip below it, urgency kicks in until you return to your baseline. But once you ease up, complacency creeps in, and things revert to the usual. To grow, you must continually raise that zero line by challenging your standards.

- We don't rise to the level of our expectations; we fall to the level of our standards.

- Raising your zero line means elevating your consistent way of thinking, deciding and acting. By committing to a higher standard, you'll generate new and better results.

- Money is a unit of choice.

CHAPTER 2

IT'S NOT ALL RAINBOWS AND UNICORNS

Success in investing isn't just about learning what you should be doing in your portfolio, such as understanding what direction you should pursue, what specific actions you should take, what assets to buy or income streams to generate, and what modes of thinking can accelerate your wealth and help you make better decisions.

Investing success is equally about understanding how to avoid the expensive mistakes that can cost far more than just money. Learn from those who have come before you and begin to understand where investors get stuck, where they go wrong, what contributes to the missteps and how they recover.

Let me let you in on a little secret: your journey isn't aways going to be rainbows and unicorns. Things will go wrong. Anticipate it, accept it and move on. It is your ability to dust yourself off, reassess, refocus and keep building that will dictate whether you succeed or fail as an investor.

We all know that our greatest challenges often become our greatest learnings, and this is where self-awareness meets wealth building. That's certainly been my experience. Goodness I've stuffed some things up, but I got back up, dusted myself off and kept building.

I want you to be able to withstand whatever challenges come your way, to stay strong in a storm, rebuild when needed, grow and expand when the time is right, and ultimately to become truly empowered, so money becomes merely a tool that permits you to live a full life and do good in the world.

On the journey toward investing success, be a student of your own experiences and those of others who came before you. Learn these lessons, so you don't repeat the same mistakes.

I'll share a few of my own with you here.

Broken and broke

Before I got into the world of investing I was a personal trainer working long hours, desperately trying to get ahead. By age 19 I felt burnt out. I'd spent the past year falling sick repeatedly because I was overworking and under-resting, and my health felt broken.

After surgery on both legs due to overuse injuries from high-level sports (judo at the time), my body too felt broken. Even my relationship felt broken because I had no time to invest in it. What's more, despite working 16-hour days, I was financially broke.

My belief about creating success at the time was very simple: the harder I worked, the more successful I'd become. It was the rule that governed much of my life.

Later I would discover that many—and I mean tens of thousands of the investors I've taught over the years—had begun by following this misguided rule until, like me, they had come to the powerful realisation that this societal norm leads only to a life of thankless hard work.

Getting to your done moment

It was December 15, 2002, at 9 am when I had my 'done moment'. A done moment in your life is the instant when you find you cannot tolerate another moment of the status quo. You're done.

I was running yet another fitness bootcamp in Kangaroo Point in Brisbane and had been driving willing participants up and down the long, winding staircase running up the side of the cliffs. After everyone had dispersed, I was having a quiet moment to myself sitting on top of those cliffs, looking out at the city and reflecting on the year drawing to a close.

I took a long hard look at my life and my honest assessment had me asking myself, *Is this all there is?* I thought about what my life might look like in five years or ten years if I kept following the same path, and I had this sick feeling in my stomach.

I didn't have the words for it at the time, but I knew instinctively that If I kept playing by the same set of rules I was going to land myself directly in the middle. And I knew I wanted more. More time, more freedom, more choices, more meaning.

That day I made one of those done decisions that change the direction of your life. The kind of decision that sees you leave all your excuses behind you and truly commit to a new pathway.

I realised I could have results or I could have excuses, but I couldn't have both.

Perhaps you've made a similar kind of decision, in this or another area of your life. You reached a point where you drew a line in the sand and committed to a new set of outcomes, and you never looked back. Perhaps it centred on a relationship or your health or a career direction? Maybe you are at a point on your financial journey right now where you're looking for another pathway?

The experience set me on a journey to finding a new set of rules to follow. I wanted to know how other people got ahead, to learn their secret. How did others make it when I couldn't?

There are no secrets to success, only systems

What I found interesting was that, to my surprise, there was no secret. Successful people were not just born under a lucky star or blessed with some innate genius that I lacked. They weren't gifted a lot of money or brought up with some extraordinary privilege.

Successful people just followed a different set of rules, so they achieved different results. They were operating in life and in business and in money using a different system from mine, and I wanted to understand it.

This launched me on my quest to understand what makes the difference in people's lives. What were the ways of thinking, the habits, the consistent actions and commitments that made all the difference to their results? This became the focus of my study.

One thing I discovered on my quest was that the wealthy and successful lacked one notable rule in their system that most other people, including myself at the time, lived by. It was relying only on the 'exchanging time for money' equation as their mode of wealth creation. That was absent, gone, eliminated.

I realised then that if I continued to base my capacity for success and earning on how many hours I put in, my results were always going to be limited. After all, we only have so much time in our day.

The big lesson was that if I didn't get my money working hard for me, then I was going to spend my entire life just working hard for money.

Now don't get me wrong. I fully believe in working hard towards what you want in life. But if it's your *only* strategy, you'll end up stuck, exhausted and burnt out—just as I was.

Profits are better than wages

So who is working harder in your life—you or your money?

The first property I ever purchased cemented this lesson for me. At age 20 I threw caution to the wind and made a decision to buy my first home in six months' time. A solid goal, right?

A tiny problem arose right away, though: I had no money! Which made my plan kind of difficult to bring off. But I had made the decision, and I now had a choice: I had to either find a way to make it happen or look for excuses for why I couldn't.

I chose option one and started scrimping and saving on lifestyle spending. I also found ways to increase my income while putting money away. Six months later I had saved a little over $9000.

I know it doesn't sound much, but at the time it felt like a fortune. Unfortunately, $9000 wasn't enough to land my first deal. However, I still followed through with my decision. With a first homeowner's grant, stamp duty savings and a 97 per cent loan from the bank, I managed to carry it over the line. My first investment property cost me $291 500—I had done it! I was out of money, but I had acquired a property.

In the following six months I saved another $10 000 to do a renovation on the property. And nine months after I had bought this first property I was able to get it revalued and pull out $72 000 of equity—in less than a year.

I had just made more than my annual income on a single property deal. And I had learned a very valuable lesson: as the late Jim Rohn would argue, *profits are better than wages*. This was my introduction to what I now consider one of the key principles of wealth creation and success in any area of life—leverage.

By leveraging the money, time, experience and wisdom of others, you can create results far greater than would be possible by yourself.

Surround yourself with wealth

Needless to say, that was a turning point in my life. I was hooked on investing!

I immediately reassessed everything in my life. I got out of personal training, the army, university, everything. I wanted to immerse myself in this new world. I began working with mentors as I made my move towards securing my second property. I joined coaching programs to learn about shares and options trading, and I began studying for my real estate licence.

Within two weeks of collecting my real estate certificate I landed my first job as a fresh-faced real estate agent to begin building up my experience in the industry, and to be around others who loved investing and believed the same things I did.

I was in for a rude shock. Out of 17 agents in our office, only one other owned an investment property. WTF?

Clearly it wasn't the right place for me. I knew I had to surround myself with people who could support who I was choosing to become and who were in alignment with my dreams. Today I call this 'building your ecosystem of wealth', and I believe it is one of the missing pieces of the puzzle in a lot of people's wealth goals. (Later we will design yours together.)

Normal, in life, is working to pay the bills for 40+ years. It is the financial ecosystem most of us are indoctrinated in and it leads to a life of financial slavery. Paying the bills, paying the rent or mortgage, paying away your money in taxes and saving for a rainy day—this is the norm, the middle.

What if instead you normalise wealth creation in your life? Where investing and being on top of your finances and building your way towards financial freedom are as normal to you as paying a bill? What kind of environment would that create and how would it support your financial growth and your journey out of the middle? It's an important mindset shift.

I wanted to build my ecosystem of wealth. So I began calling my property mentors weekly, sometimes more often, in search of opportunities. I wanted to begin working with them. And after perhaps six months of calls and emails, having annoyed them enough and convinced them I wasn't going away, they relented and made me a job offer.

Now I was in the world I wanted to be in ... and loving it!

It's not about the asset

My portfolio and my wealth began to grow quickly. I was investing in multiple asset classes and had learned how to create mini wealth systems, and I was enjoying watching the results compound.

I never got stuck on one asset class during any of my investment career. I found that this was a limiting factor in many investors' portfolios. Almost every asset class can serve a purpose within a well-constructed portfolio.

As much as I love all these asset classes, at a fundamental level investing is never about individual assets, which are simply vehicles for creating a financial result. They are cogs in a system that can help people live a better lifestyle. In later chapters I'll go into greater detail about the different asset classes and how to go about choosing them based on your risk profiles and needs, as well as the strategies to deploy to build a strong financial fortress.

Wealth building is a marathon, not a sprint

Was my portfolio perfect? Hell no, as I was about to find out the hard way.

My focus as a young investor was on accumulating more and more assets, as at the time that's what I thought investing was all about. 'How can I get to my next deal?' This was the only question I was even attempting to answer at the time, little realising I was missing most of the game.

Don't get me wrong, things were great at first. Every deal I made helped fund my next project. I made good trades, expanded my portfolio and soon my ego was swelling as quickly as my portfolio. I honestly thought I was the chosen one as an investor.

There was, however, a problem. Unknowingly I had built a house of cards in my portfolio, and I failed to protect myself by building on deep and strong foundations. Foundations of solid financials, solid structuring, solid lending principles, solid and comprehensive strategy, and solid cashflow management. Once the economic winds blew in the wrong direction I lost everything.

I learned first-hand that making mistakes in investing can be very expensive—financially, in the time spent trying to figure it out on your own, in the stress it can cause and in the potential lost opportunity. As I have often seen, the latter can be the biggest expense of all.

Having to start all over again was one of my most painful and humbling experiences. But equally it was one of the most important for me as an investment coach and strategist. It made me hypersensitive about protecting people, families and their portfolios.

Don't make the goal of wealth building all about how much you can make or how quickly you can make it. As I discovered, that just builds a house of cards. Rather, make your wealth building equally about how much of your wealth you can keep. It's about building *sustainable wealth*.

Build wealth based on you

Should you be following the same rules I did or a different pathway?

I have a core belief that every single person has a genius. Not be the type of genius we are taught to strive for in school, but rather the innate characteristics and qualities that make you who you are. And it is by understanding how to tap into and leverage them that you can enter the inside lane to your success.

I call this your *wealth genius*. Think of it as your path of least resistance to wealth. Although there is the system for wealth creation, it's how you personalise that system that will determine how fast or slow you progress.

I don't subscribe to a one-size-fits-all approach to wealth building. It doesn't work. The reality is we are all different, which is one reason why I'm often frustrated in the investment education space. You see 'gurus' up on stage peddling their own methodology, whether it be on options, trading, developing property or renovating.

I've seen too many people caught up in the hype of one course or another, yet quite unable to convert the experience into solid results. Sometimes that happens because they didn't follow through with the actions required. For others, the approach simply didn't align with who they are—their natural gifts, risk profile, personality, stage in life, decision-making style and so on.

We are taught in life to 'fix our weaknesses'. This is a pathway to mediocrity and the middle and, frankly, just hard work. What we should be doing instead is doubling down on our strengths.

Have you ever felt like you're forever pushing a boulder uphill and life is just a grind? It might be a sign that you are on the wrong path and it's time to stop and rethink!

On the flip side, we've probably all experienced times when everything feels effortless and in flow. Other people look at us and ask, 'How did you do that?' or 'You made that look so easy!' They may even say, 'You're so lucky' when you achieve a certain result. What you may not realise is that these moments leave clues for you. It's worth noting what you were doing at the time, how it felt, how you were thinking and what result you created.

You need to follow the breadcrumbs from your own life.

We can create our greatest momentum when we learn to understand ourselves at a deeper level and to tap into and apply our gifts. Most people don't talk about self-awareness and investing together, but to me this is essential; after all, you are your greatest wealth-building vehicle.

I remember exactly when I first began to recognise and understand this concept. I was in Byron Bay spending time with some friends over new year. These were no ordinary hangout gatherings. We would use the time to challenge each other and grow, and we'd bring in cool people to share their own genius so we could learn from them. One of them was just incredible at unpacking personality profiling. Her debrief of my results was so accurate I felt like I'd been found out! She aced what I was great at, what I found challenging and was downright terrible at, my ways of thinking, how I made decisions and saw the world, and so much more. This deeper understanding changed everything for me in terms of how I communicate, handle relationships, build teams, build wealth and grow businesses.

I've since helped many investors discover more about themselves and use this understanding to lay out their own personalised pathway to wealth building. What might your genius be and how might you double down on it to access your path of least resistance to wealth? After all, we do best at what we *enjoy* doing.

What does freedom mean to you?

Where is it all heading? Where does this unique path to wealth creation lead? Like your wealth journey, your ultimate destination of financial freedom will also be unique to you.

What if you were to unpack what your version of financial freedom really means to you and how much it would cost? What kind of clarity might that bring?

I have broken down financial freedom into three elements. Use these as a thinking framework that allows you to personalise your financial freedom. This is useful for getting clear on your destination so you can begin aligning your thoughts and actions towards it. It will also help you when calculating your financial freedom figure (more on this in chapter 4).

Following are the three frameworks for your financial freedom.

1. Experience of life

Financial freedom lets you fully experience life without being limited by your income. We live in a beautiful world, and there's so much to enjoy and experience. What a tragedy to be denied such opportunities for lack of funds.

Think about:
- pursuing an experience that makes you grin from ear to ear
- exploring a destination that makes your heart sing
- witnessing an event that makes your jaw drop in awe.

2. Pursuit of purpose

Financial freedom gives you the freedom to pursue your passions and purpose and find deeper meaning, because life is about so much more than working to pay the bills. Retirement is a middle-style goal; what if instead of focusing on retirement you focused on designing a life you don't have to retire from?

Think about:
- what you would be doing with your time, if money was no object

- what you are deeply passionate about
- what your greater purpose is, if you already know.

3. Creating a legacy

Financial freedom allows you to create a legacy. Most people I meet want to give back to the world and contribute to something they believe in, but their ability to do so is often limited by their time, money, energy or knowledge. What if money and time were unlimited? How might you choose to leave the world in a better place?

Think about:

- something you care about deeply that you want to influence in this life
- a cause you are passionate about that you would love to support in some way
- how you might leave your wealth to future generations.

Earlier in the chapter I mentioned that investing isn't about the actual asset you choose as your vehicle, but rather about the purpose it serves within your portfolio. Equally, financial freedom isn't about the money you make, but rather the choices it gives you to live a fuller life.

It is this journey you are here to embrace. Now let's talk about the new set of rules you're going to need to adopt to get there.

Power points

- If hard work is your only strategy, it will lead you to a life of financial slavery.

- You can have results or excuses, but you can't have both.

- There are no secrets to success, only systems.

- If you don't get your money working hard for you, you will spend your whole life working hard for money.

- Leveraging money, time, and the experience and wisdom of others allows you to achieve results far greater than you alone could accomplish.

- Consciously design your ecosystem of wealth—don't leave it to chance.

- Investing is not about any individual asset; each is just a cog in an overarching wealth system designed to create an outcome.

- Wealth building is a marathon, not a sprint.

- Wealth building isn't just about how much money you make; it's also about how much money you *keep*.

- Making mistakes in investing is expensive. It costs money, time, energy and—often most costly of all—lost opportunity.

- Your personal wealth genius is your path of least resistance to wealth.

- Don't focus on fixing your weaknesses; instead, learn to double down on your strengths. This is where your greatest source of leverage lies.

- There is no one-size-fits-all approach to wealth building. Capture the framework but personalise it to your unique genius.

- You are your greatest wealth-building asset worthy of investment and focus.

- Financial freedom has three primary elements:

  1. the freedom to fully experience life unlimited by your income

  2. the freedom to pursue your passions and purpose rather than only working to pay the bills

  3. the freedom to create your legacy and build wealth that outlasts you, so the world is a better place because you were here.

CHAPTER 3

IN THE GAME

How are you playing the money game right now? Let's start with the obvious. Following the traditional path of 'get a job and work hard' is not the best strategy to win the game of money. Sadly, it's the only path most of us are taught to follow as we step into the game, but it risks leaving us stuck, broke and exhausted, an NPC in the money game of life.

I was introduced to NPC, for 'non-player character', while watching a Ryan Reynolds movie with my daughter. It's a term used in gaming for characters who are part of the story but are not actual players and cannot control their own actions. They might be a shopkeeper, a comrade in a shooter game or a magical being who hands out quests. They don't level up like a player might, they don't evolve and they can't win the game. Instead, they are stuck in a programmed loop that dictates what they do and say.

Meet Blue Shirt Guy

Free Guy tells the story of Guy, an ordinary joe living in Free City. Guy follows exactly the same routine every day, wears the same clothes, orders the same coffee (cream and two sugars) from the same barista and walks past the same shop-window display of shoes he can't afford. He meets his best friend Buddy in the same spot on the way to his job as a bank teller, where every single day there is a bank robbery by one of the Sunglasses People.

Guy's life unreels exactly the same way every day, just as it does for all the other NPCs of Free City. But for the Sunglasses People, life is different. They can do whatever they want, whether it's parachuting out of helicopters, robbing banks, blowing things up, stealing cars or engaging in various other reckless activities.

To Guy, this is just the way life is. He knows he can't do the things the Sunglass People do; somehow, they are different, unique, special. Like the other NPCs, Guy accepts that this is their reality. After all, it's how they are programmed and all they have ever known.

Then one day Guy comes across the woman of his dreams and his entire way of life and programming is interrupted. He begins to question everything. His friends notice his change of behaviour and can't understand it.

One morning Guy enters his usual coffee shop and orders a cappuccino instead of the usual cream and two sugars. The whole shop stops and everyone stares at him as though he's an alien or criminal. In a moment of panic, Guy relents to the social pressure, pretends he was joking and orders his usual—and immediately everyone relaxes.

Guy has seen too much, though, and can no longer follow the same path and unthinkingly abide by the societal norms of Free City. In a desperate moment he snatches a pair of sunglasses from one of the players, and as he puts them on a whole new world opens up—one that had always been there but had been hidden from him. A world with different rules, where players could live a very different kind of life, with more money, more freedom, more possibilities than he had ever imagined.

Guy begins to learn the rules of how to play the new game and levels up as a character in order to succeed in this world. When he discovers he is an NPC in a game he sets out to save his virtual world from being permanently deleted and to free his fellow NPCs.

Guy becomes the hero of his own story by thinking differently, taking risks and challenging the status quo. He breaks free from complacency and no longer accepts the way things are, and he reaps the rewards both personally and in his ability to help others break free too.

Life in the middle can feel a lot like what Guy experienced before he broke free, where every day is the same as the last and every day ahead will likely be the same too.

Have you been playing the money game like an NPC, blindly following the set program laid out by society, or have you already slipped on a pair of sunglasses to prepare yourself to win the game? It's time to choose how you're going to show up.

Choose your mode

When we think about people and money, it's easy to fall into the trap of categorising them based solely on their economic class or how much money they have. Personally, I find this perspective to be of limited value, especially in a world where many already carry the weight of various challenges. The last thing we should do is confine people to such narrow labels.

This isn't to say you should lie to yourself, soften your approach to how you look at your current situation and pretend it's okay when, if you are honest with yourself, it really isn't.

Here's the tough love part. Call a spade a spade, get real with yourself and your situation. If an aspect of your financial life is stagnating, say it, own it, take responsibility for it, then do something about it. Making yourself feel better in the moment by fooling yourself and others serves no one. It just keeps you trapped in a space of false complacency, pretending everything is okay.

Your financial success has as much to do with your mindset as it does your financial strategies, a topic we will dive deeper into in chapter 7.

You will find people who, though they don't have a lot of money right now, show up in the world of money with a wealthy and abundant mindset. And by focusing their energies on the outcome they want, they can change objective reality to meet their ambitions.

Conversely, we have all heard of the big Lotto winners who lose it all in a few short years. This is because their mode of thinking and acting didn't change to meet their new circumstances and in the end they fell back into their default behaviour.

We know of people with very limited financial resources who are among the happiest in the world because they live in a space of gratitude and curiosity. What an abundant way to approach life!

We also know of people who have all the advantages in the world, yet who struggle to find happiness in life and are unable to find gratitude.

More important than how much money you have is your mode of thinking when it comes to money and wealth, and how you show up for your money life.

There are four main money modes in the money game of life:

1. Survival mode
2. Middle mode
3. Momentum mode
4. Abundance mode.

Understanding each of these modes will help you identify the way in which you're currently showing up in your money life. Ask yourself what is keeping you stuck, and what new level of thinking is required to move to the next level.

Let's review each of these modes and what they mean, then it will be time for you to look at each area of wealth and define some clear action steps.

Money mode #1: Survival

For most of us, what we learn in school doesn't adequately prepare us for the rest of our lives. When we finish, we're thrown into a sea of work, financial challenges, responsibilities and temptations, and countless other distractions, and left to figure everything out for ourselves.

We know we're supposed to swim and swim hard, but the problem is we've never been taught how. So we slip into the first of the money modes—Survival mode.

In survival mode it can feel like you're drowning in all the financial demands of life, with bill after bill and expense after expense in waves lapping over your head. You keep kicking towards the surface. Your legs are churning as you tread water. You're going nowhere fast, just trying to stay afloat, praying that a bigger wave doesn't come along and force you under again.

As you look around, often all you can see is the water right in front of your face, then the bobbing heads of others in the crowded sea around you, all treading water and, like you, struggling to stay afloat.

Many people live their entire lives at this financial waterline simply because they were never taught how to swim.

Focus of the survivors

Survivors are stuck in the 'work to pay the bills' financial slavery trap. Their focus is on sustaining themselves, putting food on the table, keeping a roof over their heads and trying not to drown financially.

What got you here

You followed the default life path—school, study hard, get a safe secure job, buy lots of stuff you don't need, get credit cards and continue to exchange time for money your entire life.

What's keeping you stuck

You're generally too busy, tired and distracted to consider if there might be a better way. Many believe the only solution to financial problems is more hard work. It's a chicken-and-egg dilemma: you need more time to make more money, and you need more money to buy back some of your time.

You're far from alone here, and yes it's daunting to be stuck in this cycle, but know that there's always a way out! If others have done it, you can too.

Consequences of staying here

Imagine an entire life spent working to pay bills, never living out your greatest passions and potential, never being able to fully explore the world around you or making the contribution you could, enslaved by your job, eventually retiring on the pension or penny pinching to make sure you have enough money to make it through.

The big leap

Learn to swim and begin building your financial foundations:

- Get out of reaction mode.
- Get a financial education.
- Install a personal finance system.
- Rewire your mindset.

Money mode #2: Middle

You've learned to swim and to navigate the financial currents of life, even if it's with a quirky doggy paddle, which is all you've managed so far. But at least you're not drowning in debt or financial stress. You've found some rhythm in your life, even if it doesn't quite match the dream life you envisioned.

Many others are doggy paddling around you, all heading in the same direction. You wonder if anyone leading the group knows where they're going. Still, you think, everyone else is doing it, so it must be right.

It's exhausting, though. Your arms ache and you're out of breath. You've been swimming with this pack for years, maybe decades, hoping to reach some destination. At least you're not just treading water anymore, as you used to. Your income is stable, you have a mortgage and some savings.

Yet you're still paddling hard, unsure of your destination, feeling stuck in the middle. It's not bad, but you had thought there was more to life. Real freedom still feels out of reach.

Still, something interesting happens now and then. You notice someone cruising effortlessly through the centre of the pack. It seems like the way just opens up for them.

What do they know that you don't?

Some resent these faster swimmers, blaming them for being careless or selfish, while others say they're just lucky. Some share inspiring stories of those who found land. You can't help but wonder: How did they swim so fast? What do they know that you don't?

Focus of the middle mode

People in middle mode often prioritise attaining comfort, predictability and security. Yet they experience a seemingly endless stream of wants. There's always something new they feel they 'need', which creates a sense of being on a never-ending chase.

This strong drive for comfort makes change scary, and herein lies the curse of the middle: fear. Fear of change, fear of losing what they have, fear of not having enough, fear of not looking successful to others, fear of failing... fear can paralyse progress.

What got you here

Following the default life path as you were taught has landed you in the middle. At the core of this mode is a deeply ingrained 'just work hard' mentality as the primary means of achieving success and financial stability.

Middle mode engenders many competing forces, both physical and psychological, which can make it a sticky trap. Consider the competition between keeping a roof over your family's head, food on the table and some money saved for a rainy day versus buying things so as to look and feel good now. Or the desire to get ahead financially versus the mixed messages about work–life balance. Or making strong, future-based financial decisions versus keeping up with the Joneses. It's no wonder manoeuvring your way out can be challenging.

What's keeping you stuck

- **Becoming the bottleneck.** Relying on a time-for-money strategy limits your success to the hours in a day, making you the bottleneck—unless you learn to leverage your time and resources.
- **Wanting to fit in.** The need to fit in leads you to blindly follow societal norms and ultimately to prioritise others' opinions over financial success.
- **Choosing stability.** The priority of keeping things the same as opposed to taking advantage of opportunities for growth and expansion means you prioritise stability over success.
- **Complacency.** The middle can be a dangerous place where things aren't bad enough to force change but aren't great enough to bring true happiness, leading to complacency.
- **Choosing balance over freedom.** Modern life brings with it a constant push–pull between working hard to buy things and achieving the ever-elusive work–life balance. This is why reclaiming your freedom is essential, one freedom at a time (more on this later).
- **Choosing instant vs delayed gratification.** In an age of instant gratification, we often want things now without considering the long-term impact this may have. Mastering money is a long game requiring patience, strategy and learning from failure.
- **The 'one day when' syndrome.** Time is the most used and abused excuse of all. Many talk about not having

enough time, while others push time back: 'I'll begin investing one day when the kids are grown or the economy picks up or my boss gives me a raise or I've finally paid off the mortgage or I have more time or I've saved more money...' There are countless *one day when* excuses. What's your favourite?

Consequences of staying here

We fall into a monotonous routine, reliving the same day for 40 years, waiting for Fridays, paydays, and that magical destination when we can retire and live the vaunted good life. Staying here is akin to giving up on your dreams for comfort now.

You may indeed find comfort here, but are you comfortable with your results? You will have to make a choice between comfort and change. Most people choose comfort and remain stuck in the middle, wishing and hoping for something different.

The big leap

- Transition from being a consumer who spends money on goods and services to an investor who strategically grows and compounds their wealth.
- Be prepared to swim away from the pack, even if others don't understand your motives.
- Seek out mentors or peer groups who are pursuing the different paths that you want to be on.
- Start shifting your focus to having your money work hard for you, rather than spending your life working hard for money. In short, get invested. And, of course, continue the foundation-building work, which never ends.

Money mode #3: Momentum

Curious, you begin to move to the edge of the pack for a better view. Perhaps you advance to the front as you become a stronger swimmer, or maybe you shift to the side to escape the splashing and see more clearly.

You start to notice more of the faster swimmers around you. Some even ride on kayaks or jet skis, and occasionally a big yacht sails swiftly by. And you come to realise that after all they might not be as rare as unicorns; they're not gods, but just ordinary people who have chosen a different path.

You begin to emulate the faster swimmers, observing how they move and what they say to themselves and to others, or even to you if you muster the courage to approach them. And you find that most are happy to talk and offer pointers to help you progress faster or share tools to assist you along the way. In fact, they turn out to be nothing like how they were described back in the middle.

You've learned that finding land isn't just a pipe dream. It's quite possible to build your own house of wealth on a firm foundation. You've been offered directions. Along the way, you may acquire fins to speed up your stroke and find a supportive squad to cheer you on.

The middle pack falls further behind as you adopt better financial strategies and grow your investment portfolio, bringing the shoreline closer. You can see the bottom of the ocean now and all at once your feet touch the bottom perhaps for the first time.

This is the financial foundation you've built, deep and strong, allowing you to walk up the gentle slope towards dry land. Your future, full of possibilities and opportunities, is waiting. There's still work to do, but the firm footing gives you confidence and momentum. Now it's time to learn a new set of skills as you begin to understand what it means to build your new home on the island.

Focus of the momentum mode

Momentum mode is a period of significant transformation in both thought and action. You are breaking away from old patterns and choosing to leave behind previous patterns of thought, interaction and behaviour in the financial game of life.

What got you here

Courage! The courage to break free from the pack, to think and act differently, regardless of what others think, to seek help from those who have walked this path before you, to make educated financial and investment decisions, to learn a new language of money and develop new skills, and to pursue what you want in life, refusing to settle for less than you deserve.

What's keeping you stuck

All too often people who reach the point of wanting change, and are ready to make it happen, try to go it alone without the necessary knowledge, experience, networks and systems to make safe and effective decisions.

This often leads to one of two outcomes: they procrastinate through fear and lack the confidence to take the next step; or they make rushed or uneducated decisions that result in costly mistakes. Now's the time to seek help and mentorship. By setting up a strong wealth foundation, with guidance you can leapfrog forward in your results.

Entering this new world can lead to a yo-yo effect: you take a step forward, then a step back and repeat. This happens because there's an internal battle between your old money habits and the new ways of thinking you're adopting as you raise your zero line and move to the next level.

Consequences of staying here

An important one is unrealised potential. You had a glimpse of it—you could see the possibilities and your future waiting for you, but something held you back from moving from momentum to abundance. Was it fear? Complacency? Did you take your foot off the pedal, or did excuses creep back in?

The big leap

- **Get a mentor.** A mentor is your fast track to success. Tap into the experience and knowledge of someone who has already walked this path. They can help you take effective steps forward and avoid costly mistakes. The good news is you're already doing this right now by reading this book!

- **Create a peer group.** It can feel lonely walking this path at times. Self-doubt, complacency and old programming can easily creep in. Having a supportive peer group around you can be both an accelerator and a source of support when you need it most.

- **Develop a strategy.** Building wealth requires more than just buying a few assets; it's about creating a cohesive portfolio that works as a system to guide you towards financial freedom. I share some of these strategies later in the book.

Money mode #4: Abundance

It's time to acquire a new set of skills as you adjust to life on land and start envisioning what you want to build on your island.

You've achieved so much on your journey to this point in your life—don't stop now. Start outlining your plans, gathering materials and tools, and establishing a structure for growth. With the financial education you've accumulated, which continues to expand, your confidence in making effective financial decisions, and the support network and team you've built, financial freedom is no longer a pipe dream; if you stay the course, it's inevitable.

You already have a financial foundation, but you know that the deeper and stronger that foundation, the more abundant your vision can be, so you continue intentionally strengthening it.

With the right strategies in place, you begin intentionally constructing buildings, each one flowing seamlessly into the next as you create your own self-sufficient cashflow-producing fortress.

You might even own some seafaring vessels now, granting you access to tools and resources that are not available on your current island. Perhaps you've even felt called to return to guide swimmers who seek your help.

You remember your frantic swimming days vividly. Honestly, it's hard to relate to the person you were then; your level of thinking and life experiences have evolved significantly. You've become a different person.

Empowered knowledge

You know what is possible. Even if a giant wave were to wash over your island and topple a building or two, you know how to rebuild.

You know what it's like to breathe easy and leverage off assets, and you have systems to handle the heavy lifting, rather than relying solely on hard work and dedicated hours. Your life's course is no longer dictated by others—whether it be a boss, the government, a location or societal norms. You are in command.

Focus of the abundance mode

A key to the shift from momentum to abundance mode is an expanded mindset. Your sense of what's possible for your finances and future grows, moving beyond the limitations often seen in survivor and middle modes.

You don't reach this level without relentless implementation. This is where I think enthusiasts of the law of attraction get it wrong. I once joined a law of attraction group on Facebook, but my stay was brief. When someone posted for everyone to write in the comments, 'I will make $10 000 by this weekend, and it will be so', the flood of emotions that erupted within me was colourful to say the least. Part of me wanted to throw up over the stupidity of it. I just wanted my time back, and to punch the person who wrote the post, because they were not serving readers at all by promoting wishful and lazy thinking without the practicalities to go alongside it to really help people.

Don't get me wrong, I'm a big believer in the law of attraction, but if it's your *only* strategy then you are just dreaming and unwilling to do the work. The law of attraction only works if you do. But if you just wish something then sit on your backside waiting for it to fall into your lap, the universe will laugh in your face, because you are not being serious.

The law of attraction works only when combined with strategic action—in other words, it works when you work for it. You need to align your head, heart and feet in the same direction. First, get clear on what you want so you have a tangible outcome and create a plan to turn your dream into reality (head). Then, deeply connect with your desired outcome—make that vision so real in your heart that you can feel it and taste it until it becomes a part of you (heart). Finally, take consistent, strategic steps towards your plan (feet).

When you align these elements, you'll see how powerful the law of attraction becomes when you work with it. This alignment signals to your unconscious mind that you're fully committed to achieving your goal. Without this level of commitment, you're simply relying on hope.

All the most beautiful strategies, education, teams and master plans will mean squat unless you implement like crazy. Perhaps there should be a money mode 3.5 GSD: Get shit done!

By this time you have moved away from 'just work hard' as your sole strategy and are instead relying on proven systems that run like clockwork to grow your assets and cashflow while keeping you safe.

What got you here

You have demonstrated incredibly virtuous traits to reach this point in your life. These include:

- **commitment.** Staying true to your decision to change your life despite challenges, naysayers and setbacks has paid off. Your commitment shows in both your results and your self-belief.
- **responsibility.** You refused to be a victim of your circumstances. Instead, you took responsibility and action to change your situation. And you didn't blame others, a key trait of the wealthy and successful.

- **strategy.** Each level requires a different strategy. The mindset, habits, actions and financial strategies that got you to one level won't necessarily work for the next. Your success has come from your ability to adapt, change and grow.

What's kept you stuck

You're not stuck. You're just growing.

Consequences of staying here

Although firmly settled into your abundance mode, you may still not be financially free, but even if you're not there just yet you are well on your way. Don't become complacent now. Take advantage of the momentum you have created to cement in your assets and income streams so deeply they can never be moved, and secure your future and legacy.

You now get to decide how far you want to go and what you want to create.

What are your goals? Financial security? Financial freedom? Empire building? Being a mentor? Building wealth and creating a legacy that outlasts you?

The big leap

Once you have secured your freedom, lock away the part of your portfolio that will secure your freedom, and liquidate the parts you will now use to build your legacy.

What mode are you in?

Have you identified which mode best reflects where you currently stand? Maybe you noticed some exceptions? For instance, you might feel stuck in survival mode in certain aspects of your financial life, while experiencing momentum or even abundance in others.

Perhaps your portfolio is in the middle mode, but your mindset has progressed to momentum, and you're working to align your financial reality with that elevated thinking. Or it could be the reverse — you've come into some money, but realise that your current habits around money management need significant improvement to catch up with your newfound resources.

What we already understand is that building wealth isn't just about accumulating assets, creating new income streams or better managing your money. It's about all of these things, and more.

Let's get more specific by briefly exploring each of these areas before diving deeper into them in later chapters. This will help you assess which mode you're operating in for each area, allowing you to recognise where you're excelling and pinpoint areas that need improvement to truly elevate your financial game.

Download the table from www.escapethemiddle.com. As you go through each of the following wealth-building accelerators, grade yourself, identifying whether you're in survival mode, middle mode, momentum or abundance mode for each one.

It all starts with shifting your *mindset* to a higher frequency of wealth building. I call this activating your 'millionaire mode'. Take a moment to reflect: Where do you feel your current mindset is when it comes to money and wealth building in your life right now?

Now it's time to focus on raising your *financial IQ* by gaining a practical, real-world financial education. How actively are you educating yourself on real-world financial strategies, and where do you believe your current financial knowledge stands? How prepared do you feel to take control of your financial future based on your current level of understanding?

We focus on maximising your *earning potential* because the more income you can feed into your wealth-building funnel, the more wealth you'll create when paired with the right strategy. So how solid is your primary source of income? How confident are you in your ability to grow it? And what steps are you currently taking to maximise its potential?

Do you have a *personal finance system* in place that methodically manages your money, ensuring every dollar has a plan and purpose, so you're never left wondering, 'Where did all my money go?' How clear, fine-tuned and automated is your system for tracking, managing and optimising your income, expenses and savings?

Do you currently have *debt*, and are you in control of it, using it strategically? Or is it controlling you? Is your debt working as a tool to help build your wealth, or is it limiting your financial growth?

Having just one *income stream* is risky, two is okay, three offers stability, and four or more is abundance mode. How many income streams do you currently have, and how secure, reliable and scalable are they?

Your financial freedom will be achieved only by owning high-quality *investment assets* that deliver real-world results for your portfolio. So do you currently have any investment assets? What is their quality? Are they aligned with your long-term financial goals, and how are they contributing to your overall wealth?

If you're relying solely on yourself on your wealth-building journey, your results may always be limited. Having the right *wealth advisory team* can give you the leverage to accelerate far beyond your own limitations. Who is currently advising or supporting you on your wealth-building path, and how confident are you in their expertise to guide you towards financial freedom?

Without a clear *wealth-building strategy*, you're essentially gambling with your financial future—and investors don't gamble! Do you have a well-defined and comprehensive strategy in place, and how effectively are you executing it?

Sustainable wealth is created by ensuring you keep what you earn and protect yourself, your family and your portfolio. This is done by establishing what I call your *financial fortress*—having the right structures in place, protection mechanisms, and ensuring your portfolio's cashflow remains strong and viable.

How well protected are your financial assets and investments? Do you feel secure with the wealth *structure* you currently have in place?

Ultimately, the goal of wealth building is to create the freedom and choices to live life on your own terms. How much personal and financial freedom are you currently experiencing, and what's holding you back from fully living life on your own terms?

So where are you on each of these pillars? Time to self-assess (see table 3.1). Download this table from www.escapethemiddle.com and complete, or simply draw it on a piece of paper. Go through each wealth building area and give yourself an honest self assessment about which mode you are currently operating within—Survival, Middle, Momentum or Abundance?

Table 3.1: a wealth-building self-assessment

Wealth-building area	Survival	Middle	Momentum	Abundance
Mindset				
Financial IQ				
Earning potential				
Personal finances				
Debt				
Income streams				
Assets				
Team				
Strategy				
Structure				

Having completed your self-assessment, what is the primary mode you feel you are currently operating in? What is the next mode you are aiming towards? And what new way of thinking is going to help you level up?

Einstein suggested a definition of insanity as doing the same thing over and over again and expecting different results. Have you shown signs of madness in your life to date—hoping things will change yet continually following the same pathway you always have? This is your chance to start on a different path. If you want to create a brand-new level of results in your financial life, you must begin showing up at a higher level than you are right now.

The opportunity is right in front of you, waiting for you to start swimming towards it.

Power points

- Just following the traditional path of 'get a job and work hard' will never help you win the game of money.

- Be honest with yourself about your financial situation. If it's not where you want it to be, take full responsibility, own it and take action to improve it. Pretending it's okay or making light of the situation will not serve you.

- Your financial success depends as much on your mindset as on your financial strategies.

- There are four main money modes in the money game of life:

  1. Survival mode

  2. Middle mode

  3. Momentum mode

  4. Abundance mode.

  Recognising which mode you are currently in will help you to understand where you are, how you got here, what's keeping you stuck, and the mindset and actions needed to reach the next level.

- The *law of attraction* only works if you work with it. You have to get your head, your heart and your feet all moving in the same direction towards your desired outcome.

- Even the best strategies, education, teams and plans are meaningless unless you implement them through relentless action.

- There are 10 areas of wealth creation required to build a wealth-building system:

  1. Shift your **mindset** to a higher frequency of wealth building. I call this activating your *millionaire mode*.

  2. Raise your **financial IQ** by gaining a practical, real-world financial education.

  3. Maximise your **earning potential**, as more income channelled into your wealth-building funnel generates greater wealth when paired with the right strategy.

  4. Install a **personal finance system** that manages your money methodically, ensuring every dollar has a plan and purpose, so you're never left wondering, 'Where did all my money go?'

  5. If you are using **debt** and financial leverage, is it the type of debt that's helping build your wealth, or is it holding back your financial growth?

  6. Grow multiple **income streams**. Having just one income stream is risky, two is okay, three offers stability and four or more signals abundance mode.

  7. Assess your current asset position as your financial freedom will only be achieved by owning high-quality **investment assets** that deliver real-world results for your portfolio.

  8. Having the right **wealth advisory team** can give you the leverage to accelerate far beyond your own limitations.

9. Craft a clear wealth-building **strategy**, as without it you're essentially gambling with your financial future—and investors don't gamble!

10. Sustainable wealth is built by keeping what you earn and protecting yourself, your family and your portfolio. This is achieved by creating a **financial fortress**—establishing proper structures and protection mechanisms, and ensuring strong, viable cashflow in your portfolio.

- The goal of wealth building is to create the freedom and choices to live life on your own terms.

PART II

FACE UP TO YOUR FINANCES

CHAPTER 4

FACE UP

You have just completed a brief self-assessment on 10 complementary pillars of wealth building. How do you feel now? Was the process challenging? Was it a cause for celebration? Or maybe it did not stir much emotion at all.

As you continue through this book, it's valuable to reflect on why certain feelings or thoughts may have surfaced. These reactions can offer important insights into your beliefs around money and wealth, and can provide clues to the underlying mindset shaping your financial behaviour, allowing you to look beneath the surface of your relationship with money.

We'll explore this further in chapter 7, where we dive into the mindset and beliefs behind your financial decisions, then help you craft a new level of thinking to accelerate your financial outcomes.

This is all about *facing up to your finances*, an essential but often challenging part of mastering the money game of your life. The truth is, for most people the only time they confront their money life is in one of four instances: when there is a bill to pay; at tax time, when the government wants their piece; in an emergency when it's panic stations; or when it's too late and you feel like you've run out of time.

Hardly being in control of your financial life, wouldn't you say? This is why you must face up to your finances if you want to break free from the middle and plan and execute your escape to freedom.

In the next three chapters we'll talk about the key steps you need to take to face up:

- Lift your head up from the busyness of life to focus on something bigger and get clear on what I call your financial freedom figure.
- Take responsibility for where you are by making the 13 key investor decisions to win the money game of life.
- Execute on your strategy like a mad person and implement the number one wealth-building habit that has helped many thousands of investors take control of their finances once and for all.

Ready to face up? Let's go.

Busyness is a low standard

Being busy is the easiest thing in the world. An infinite number of distractions vie for our attention. There's a big difference between being busy and being effective, however.

It doesn't mean you're not working hard. In fact, you might be working extremely hard, but are you being intentional with what you're working hard towards? Or are you just following the crowd in the ocean of life, forever pursuing small distractions instead of your big dreams?

I used to wear my busyness like a badge of honour. Whenever someone asked, 'How are you?' I'd proudly respond, 'I'm so busy', as if it was something to be admired. I still catch myself saying it, but now it makes me pause and reflect, *Am I just being busy, or am I actually being effective?*

The key is to *begin with an end in mind.* How are you going to grow your portfolio and wealth intentionally for the future?

What does financial freedom mean to you?

Don't start with the money; start with the meaning. In discussions around money and goal setting, people talk a lot about financial freedom. What does that mean to you, though?

Some think of flashy cars and first-class travel, big homes and luxury living. Others dream of living sustainably on a piece of land, growing their own food. Neither answer is right or wrong.

Notice I didn't say anything about having a certain amount of money. The actual dollar figure you will need can come later. This is because financial freedom has nothing to do with the money itself, but everything to do with the impact it has on how you experience life. Money is just one of the tools to help you realise it.

We might redefine money as 'a unit of choice', because the more money you make, the more choices you have. Everyone's aspirations are different, which is one reason why there's no one-size-fits-all approach to wealth.

It's time to begin to understand what financial freedom means to you, because how on earth are you going to get there, if you don't know where *there* is? How will you craft a strategic wealth-building plan when you don't know what your target is?

How will you know if you are making the right decisions in the right areas, decisions that are intentionally and systematically advancing you towards your outcomes.

Here are some of the big mistakes I see people make when setting financial goals.

Mistake #1: They have none!

Without a goal, how will you know what to steer towards? You are left just 'hoping' that one day things will work out. With no clear direction to head towards, any actions you take are more or less random. You're often left sitting idle and going nowhere fast, just swept along by whatever current comes your way.

Mistake #2: They make them too big

This might seem counterintuitive, especially since the typical conversation about personal development emphasises aiming for big, ambitious goals. And while these can be valuable, helping to elevate your thinking and giving you something inspiring to work towards, the problem arises when they are your *only* focus.

Without smaller, achievable milestones to serve as stepping stones, the gap between where you are now and your ultimate goal can feel overwhelming. This can make it hard for your subconscious mind to fully commit, leading to procrastination or self-sabotage due to fear of not knowing how to get there.

Mistake #3: They make them too small

While small goals may seem manageable, they can lack the power to ignite your motivation or emotional drive or to be the catalyst that pulls you towards something greater than who and where you are in life right now.

Small, uninspiring goals can make it easy to remain complacent. Without a purpose or vision that stretches you, there's no real incentive to pursue them with passion. They don't create the emotional connection that's essential for driving sustained effort and overcoming obstacles. As a result, you may never fully commit to these goals, and they end up being more like tasks to check off a list than meaningful milestones on your path to success.

Mistake #4: They are vague and wishy-washy

When your goals are unclear and lack focus, they are difficult to achieve. Goals like 'I want to be rich' of 'I want more money' are too broad to provide any real direction. Without concrete details—such as specific numbers, deadlines or actionable steps—you don't have a clear path to follow.

Vague goals make it hard to measure progress or stay motivated, because there's nothing tangible to work towards. As a result, your efforts can become inconsistent, and it's easy to lose focus. Without clarity, you can't point your actions in a specific direction, which makes it unlikely you'll make any meaningful progress. A well-defined goal, on the other hand, creates a roadmap and keeps you accountable along the way.

Mistake #5: They have no plan to make it real

Setting a clear goal is undeniably important but it's only part of the process. Just because someone says they want a specific outcome does not mean they will achieve it. Yet many people fixate solely on the goal itself, or they try to manifest wealth and happiness through the 'law of attraction' alone.

Most people spend 95 per cent of their time focusing on setting the goal and only 5 per cent on the actions needed to achieve it. Do you see the flaw in that approach? Instead, reverse the focus. Spend 5 per cent of your time defining the goal, and 95 per cent of your time working towards making it a reality. This is where having the right system becomes crucial.

How do we break free from impotent goal setting and instead craft a set of financial goals that are not only big, beautiful and inspiring, but achievable. By setting targets that are tangible and tactical and are going to set you up to win, you become more than who you are right now.

In the end, a goal without a plan is just an idea. A plan without a goal is simply directionless effort. It may keep you busy, but it won't lead you anywhere meaningful. Both the goal and the plan must work together—one providing the destination, the other offering the roadmap.

I always tell my clients they will never out-earn themselves. If you want to level up your results in life, you have to first level up as a person and raise the standards in how you choose to play the game.

Let's start by levelling up on the wealth-building vision you have in your life with the financial freedom figure (FFF).

Setting your financial freedom figure

The big goal of setting your financial freedom figure is to give you a clear and tangible outcome that you can begin aligning your thinking, strategy and actions towards so you can build a portfolio that turns this vision into reality.

There are three key things we will be identifying in this exercise together. First, we will get clear on what financial freedom means to you. Because if you don't know what financial freedom means to you, then, in the words of Lewis Carroll, 'if you don't know where you're going and any road will take you there'.

Second, we will explore how much your financial freedom is going to cost you. Because it's all well and good having ideas about wanting more time and more things and more freedom. But if you don't have a tangible figure to work towards, how will you know what strategy you should deploy to get you to where you want to go?

Third, we will begin to get clear on what kind of portfolio you need to create to deliver the cashflow you want.

With a clear set of outcomes in place, we can reverse engineer the process all the way back to where we are right now and start to build out your roadmap to turn your dreams into reality. Think of this as the North Star by which you will to navigate towards your dream life.

The FFF pyramid

Figure 4.1 (overleaf) presents the FFF (financial freedom figure) pyramid. This is where we'll clearly and succinctly map our your very own FFF.

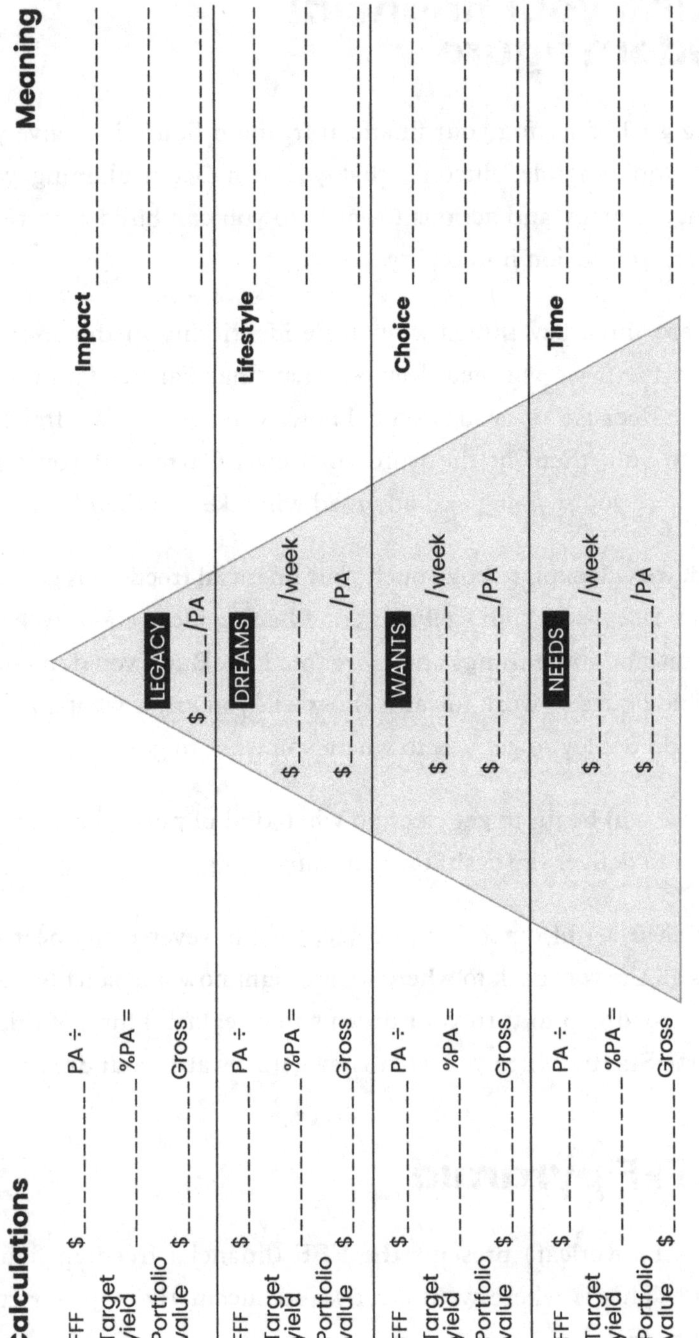

Calculations

FFF $ _____ PA ÷

Target
yield _____ %PA =

Portfolio
value $ _____ Gross

FFF $ _____ PA ÷

Target
yield _____ %PA =

Portfolio
value $ _____ Gross

FFF $ _____ PA ÷

Target
yield _____ %PA =

Portfolio
value $ _____ Gross

FFF $ _____ PA ÷

Target
yield _____ %PA =

Portfolio
value $ _____ Gross

Meaning

Impact

Lifestyle

Choice

Time

LEGACY
$ _____ /PA

DREAMS
$ _____ /week
$ _____ /PA

WANTS
$ _____ /week
$ _____ /PA

NEEDS
$ _____ /week
$ _____ /PA

Figure 4.1: the FFF pyramid

Download this template from www.escapethemiddle.com to complete for yourself.

The FFF pyramid has three key parts:

1. Inside the pyramid itself are the four levels of financial freedom—needs, wants, lifestyle and legacy.
2. On the right-hand side you will give meaning to each level.
3. On the left-hand side you will calculate how much your freedom choices will cost you and what kind of portfolio you will need to build to realise them.

Let's start building.

The four levels of financial freedom

As discussed, there are four different levels of financial freedom for you to climb. Each level will serve as a meaningful milestone towards living your dream life and creating your legacy.

We'll begin by reviewing each of these levels and mapping them out together. Don't try to make this perfect first time around. Many people allow their desire for perfection to get in the way of progress. First we want to get a messy version down, knowing that you can refine it as you continue learning and deepening your understanding.

Level 1: Your needs

The first level of your financial freedom is about creating enough income from your portfolio to cover your basic needs. Not to buy that flashy car or travel first class or give millions away—we'll get to all those juicy things as we climb up through the levels.

Right now there's one core outcome: to get your time back. Earn enough from your portfolio to cover the cost of your necessities in life so you no longer have to turn up to work just to pay the bills. Time is our most valuable asset and the more we can free up, the better.

Step 1. Add the meaning

So what does this mean to you? If you could cover your needs and you no longer had to turn up at your place of work for a wage to survive, what would you do with the time you had won?

For me, it's about having more time with family and making sure I'm not missing out on the important things with my wife and kids. I also love spending time in nature, wandering in my forest and finding new adventures.

Notice that these things don't have to cost much. The key here is to create something meaningful that would light up your life.

Step 2. Cost it out

Time to make it tangible. Notice on the second level of the pyramid there are two spaces for you to fill out, one weekly and the other annually. I include both as it is easier to think of it on a weekly basis then annualise it later so you can ultimately calculate the value of the portfolio you need to build.

How much income do you need per week to cover your basic living expenses? A question I'm often asked is whether to include your mortgage. I usually answer no, as our wealth-building plan will cover eliminating that debt. But feel free to include it if you want to err towards being conservative. After all, you're building your freedom according to your own needs and priorities.

Make sure you have annualised your figure.

Step 3. Do the sums

We'll now calculate the value of the financial freedom portfolio (FFP) you need to build in order to create the cashflow to fund your life. Here's how.

Take the annual figure that covers your needs, then divide it by the target gross yield you have for your portfolio. Your gross yield is the income you earn per annum on an asset compared to the value of the asset itself.

If you have money in the bank earning a 3 per cent interest rate, your gross yield is 3 per cent. If you have $10 000 of shares and are earning $450 per year in income, your gross yield is 4.5 per cent. If you have an investment property worth $500 000 that is earning you $480 per week, you multiply that by 52 to turn it into an annual figure. You will be earning an annual income of around $25 000. Dividing this by $500 000 will give you a 5 per cent gross yield.

Of course, you may have expenses to pay on some of these asset classes, but this just gives us the opportunity to compare apples with apples.

Typically, I target a 5 per cent gross yield for a portfolio. Some of your assets may earn more, some less, but a well-constructed portfolio should be delivering this easily.

Now time for the maths. If you set a target income of $100 000 to cover your needs and a gross yield of 5 per cent, the calculations will look like this:

$100 000 / 5% =

[drumroll please]

$2 000 000

So a $2 million portfolio owned outright yielding on average 5 per cent would provide an income of $100 000, which would cover your basic needs and win you your time back.

If you want a net income, I tend to add another 30 per cent on top of it to cover other expenses, bringing the total up to $2.6 million.

You now have a tangible figure you can build a strategy towards. It may not be 100 per cent accurate, but it is more than enough to give you a target, knowing you can refine it as you grow your portfolio and your financial and investment IQ.

How do you feel about your figure? For many people it can feel massive, and it may well be a huge jump from where you are right now, especially if you are just getting started.

What I'm going to ask you to do right now is to have faith. It might feel big because it's just not part of your normal right now. You may not have anywhere near that in your own life or may not even know anyone else who does.

Remember, we are conditioned in life to think small, to be in the middle, to focus on just working hard to pay the bills. You're simply stretching your current level of thinking from what has been your normal to date. But know that it is possible for you. I have started from the ground up and I have helped many others do the same. Just follow the system, one baby step at a time.

It's time to move on to the other levels of your financial freedom figures, and now you know the process you can go and get it done!

Level 2: Your wants

This level is the zone of 'choice'. You have already won back your time and are covering your basic living expenses. Now it's about adding in some core choices that you want to have in life.

Is it to travel every year? How much might that cost? Is it to send your kids to a private school rather than the one you can afford? How much might that require in annual school fees? Is it to give some money to family members or to a cause you want to support? Again, how much? Or perhaps you never want to have to clean your house again. How much would it cost to get a cleaner or a cook or a gardener?

Add an annual dollar figure next to it so you know how much that choice will cost you, then add them all together. Now add that to your needs figure then put it in your wants level.

Then do the maths. How much is your level two FFP value? Perhaps it adds an extra $50k on top of your needs, taking your total to $150k:

$150 000 / 5% = $3 000 000

Level 3: Your dreams

Now is the time for you to dream big. What does your dream lifestyle look like? What are all the choices you might have that would light you up? One item on my list is to dive at the most beautiful dive sites around the world. Another was to buy a home that could be fully off grid surrounded by nature and beauty, with more than enough space for my kids to make a home with their own families if they want to. I purchased this property with my wife and I couldn't be happier, but at one point this was just a dream I had.

Write them down, cost them out, add them up, tap on your wants figure and now you have it.

Perhaps it's $300 000 per annum:

$300 000 / 5% = $6 000 000

Level 4: your legacy

This is the big one for me, such that I have devoted the entire last chapter of the book to it. My goal is to leave the world in a better place than when I found it. What impact do you want to have and what legacy do you want to pass down to your family? I have goals for the intergenerational wealth I want to leave for my kids and their kids and their kids, and how I mean to make sure it's not squandered.

As a nature junkie, I have a target to purchase one million acres of land to conserve and put under trust so it's protected.

These are some of my goals, which may help stimulate your own ideas. If you have some down, work out how much they might cost and... well, you know the rest. If you're coming up empty, no problem at all. Come back to it another time.

You should now have a completed financial freedom pyramid laid out in front of you.

Your four freedom targets are in place, with the values of the FFP you'll need to build to realise each of these levels. You have meaningful exits along the way to living your ideal lifestyle and creating your legacy.

You have tangible figures to build a portfolio towards and your North Star to help pull you through the inevitable lumps and bumps of the journey.

Congratulations! How does it feel to have done this and have it sitting in front of you?

People often use words such as 'empowering' and producing 'a sense of clarity', sometimes mixed in with 'scary' and 'confronting'! Notice what words come up for you and ask yourself why you feel that way.

Okay, destination set. Now it's time to come back to the present as you front up to your situation.

Power points

- Pay attention to the emotions that arise as you grapple with the ideas in this book. These reactions can reveal important insights into your beliefs about money and wealth, helping you uncover the mindset driving your financial behaviour.

- Busyness is a low standard. Being busy is easy; the real challenge is staying effective and focusing on actions that drive results.

- Financial freedom isn't about money itself, but the impact it has on how you experience life.

- Money is a 'unit of choice'—the more you have of it, the more options you have.

- The five big financial goal-setting mistakes people make are:

  Mistake #1: They have none!

  Mistake #2: They make them too big.

  Mistake #3: They make them too small.

  Mistake #4: Their goals are vague and wishy-washy.

  Mistake #5: They have no plan to make them real.

- A goal without a plan is just an idea; a plan without a goal is aimless. Both must work together—one sets the destination, the other provides the roadmap.

- You will never out-earn yourself, so grow yourself to grow your wealth.

- The purpose of setting your financial freedom figure is to give you a clear, tangible goal to align your thinking, strategy and actions, helping you build a portfolio that makes this vision a reality. To set these goals:

1. Get clear on what financial freedom means to you.

2. Explore how much your financial freedom is going to cost you.

3. Get clear on what kind of portfolio you need to create to deliver the cashflow you want.

- There are four levels of financial freedom:

Level 1: **Needs** (zone of *time*). Create enough investment income to cover your basic living expenses to get your time back.

Level 2: **Wants** (zone of *choice*). Once you have your time back, add in the extra choices you want in your life to level up your experiences.

Level 3: **Dreams** (zone of *lifestyle*). Now is the time for you to dream big. What does your dream lifestyle look like and how much is this going to cost?

Level 4: **Legacy** (zone of *impact*). What do you want to give to your family and how do you want to leave the world a better place?

CHAPTER 5

FRONT UP

Okay, so you've lifted your head up to see your future, way beyond the middle. You've clearly defined your FFF (financial freedom figure) and identified the portfolio value required to generate the income needed to achieve your financial freedom. You may even be starting to shape ideas around what this future freedom portfolio could look like.

Now it's time to confront your current situation and take control. If you're truly committed to breaking free from the middle, building wealth and achieving financial freedom, there are some important decisions ahead. In fact, there are 14 critical decisions, all of them essential to your success as an investor. Let's run through them.

Decision #1. Commit to becoming wealthy

Your investment journey starts long before you ever put any physical cash into an investment. It begins in a single moment—perhaps it's right now, as you're reading this, or maybe it happened earlier when you chose to pick up this book. It's the moment you truly decide you're going to be wealthy in your life and burn all the bridges behind you.

Nothing moves forward until you make this decision, which is why it's the most important wealth-building decision you'll ever make.

Most people know they should be investing for the future—it's not a new science—so why do they procrastinate when it comes to making that crucial decision? It usually boils down to one simple reason: fear. It can feel intimidating to step into the unknown and take such a risk, even if it's an educated one.

Isn't this how we react to anything new? A new job may feel overwhelming at first. Starting a relationship can be intimidating, even though it brings excitement, joy, passion and all those squishy responses. Moving to a new town, starting a new hobby, learning a new skill—all such experiences felt unfamiliar and even a bit scary before they became a familiar part of your everyday life, simply because you stuck with it.

Your financial future isn't waiting for you. It's coming, whether you're ready or not. The question is, how are you preparing for it? And would you be okay if you are more or less in the same financial position as you are now in five years' time?

The cost of not investing

Many people see investing as risky, and it's true—even with the best strategy and thorough due diligence, there's always a chance of losing money. There are always forces beyond your control. But there's one thing that's riskier than investing, and that's not investing.

Consider the real cost of not taking control of your financial future and instead staying stuck in the middle, relying on the outdated financial system we were taught. The cost could be lifelong financial dependence, stuck in a job that doesn't light you up, working just to cover bills. It could be never having the freedom to pursue your passions, discover your purpose, explore the world and spend time with loved ones. It could be spending your life working then retiring near the poverty line. It could be failing to create the legacy you know you were put on this planet to pass down.

You also risk failing to teach your kids the wealth-building skills you never learned, settling for the life you can afford instead of the one you dream of. In the end, it could mean more than 90 000 hours of life spent in an unfulfilling job.

Is that cost heavy enough for you?

This is why your first decision is so crucial—it truly can't be overstated.

Decision #2. Make the decision to focus on foundations

Shiny object syndrome has probably killed more portfolios than anything else. It's exciting to invest in assets, to see the first bit of passive income roll into your bank account. But shiny object syndrome is get-rich-quick thinking. Get-rich-quick thinking leads to short-term decision making, and short-term decision making sacrifices long-term results.

Don't skip the basics in pursuit of the shiny. Instead, play the long game and keep your eyes on the prize of creating sustainable wealth that delivers consistent returns.

There are six wealth foundations to be built, we will be covering throughout the book:

1. Raise your financial IQ.
2. Set up a personal finance system.

3. Turn on your millionaire mode.
4. Construct your wealth team.
5. Build your peer group.
6. Set your strategic plan.

The stronger your foundation, the stronger your future freedom will be.

Decision #3. Make the decision to treat your financial life as a business

This critical shift in mindset must occur if you are to achieve long-term financial success. Just as a business needs to manage its finances meticulously to avoid failure, you must manage your personal wealth like a business.

If you approach your finances as a hobby, you'll get hobby-like results—sporadic, inconsistent and often disappointing. To achieve real financial success, you need to adopt a businesslike mindset. This means treating your financial life with the seriousness and strategic planning it deserves.

Decision #4. Seek real-life financial education beyond formal systems

Jim Rohn has said, 'A formal education will get you a job, self-education will make you a fortune.' The formal education system will never teach you to be free; it can't. Its job is to prepare you for the job market, to join the economic wheel of society and to be a good tax-paying citizen. In other words, to join the middle.

If you want to take control of your finances and build your wealth to create freedom, then a real-world education is essential. That's why you're here. To learn the real-life skills you should have been taught in school.

Decision #5. Build an A-team of wealth advisers with proven results

Leveraging off the expertise of others' experience and systems is an important component of wealth building, as it allows you to tap into resources well beyond your own and helps you to avoid being a bottleneck to your own success. This is where your board of wealth advisers comes into play. How you choose this team is critical, as you'll only get world-class advice from world-class experts. A word to the wise: how many qualifications they have means nothing when it comes to growing a successful investment portfolio.

Decision #6. Qualifications do not mean qualified to help you grow your wealth

This is something I feel very strongly about, and for good reason. Years back, I ran education programs teaching people how to trade options in the share market. Shares and options are considered to be financial products, so I needed to become a 'qualified' financial adviser to be allowed to teach these tactics even though I had been trading successfully for years in my own portfolio. Fair enough.

I signed up for an online course with a registered training institution and after two weekends of doing the course, I completed my open book exam with no time limit where I copied and pasted answers which primarily pertained to legalities as opposed to anything to do with wealth building and strategically advising investors. I was now 'qualified' as a financial adviser.

If you're anything like me you might be horrified by this, and to be fair, the standards have improved since that time.

When I completed my real estate licence, I learned nothing on finding property or doing due diligence or investing, I learned how to fill out contracts.

Because I spoke and coached all the time on finance when it comes to property lending, I was required to become a qualified mortgage broker and with a bit of recognition of prior learning to help me along, that course was done in a day.

I also have had many financial planners and accountants and brokers and agents as my personal clients and many have begun with no portfolios yet were still supposedly helping others to plan their finances. Go figure. Now, to their credit, they had the humility and integrity to come and learn.

Of course, there are some great financial planners and some terrible ones, as is true of accountants, nurses, doctors, builders and any profession. So this has nothing to do with diminishing the professions or the people within them, but personally I feel there should be a requirement for professionals in this space to practise what they preach, rather than just having a piece of paper saying they are qualified.

What is my point? I don't care how many qualifications someone has, it's experience that counts. Qualifications do not mean qualified to help you grow your wealth.

Choose your team wisely.

Decision #7. Learn strategically and implement effectively

The most beautifully laid out strategy is meaningless if you don't do something with it. You must implement what you know, otherwise what's the point? As Bruce Lee put it, 'Knowing is not enough, we must apply. Willingness is not enough, we must do.'

It can feel overwhelming at times when you're learning new skills, as you are now. This is why I teach my clients a simple rule to follow: *learn one thing, do one thing.* Don't get caught up in binge learning traps; focus instead on making meaningful change in your life, one step at a time.

Decision #8. Be purposeful with money

Every dollar in your life needs a plan and a purpose. Without a clear direction, money can slip through your fingers, leaving you ever further from your financial goals. When you become purposeful with money, every dollar works towards creating the future you want.

Being intentional with your money is key to building wealth. When you direct each dollar towards a specific goal—whether it's investing, saving or paying off debt—you ensure that your finances always align with your bigger picture. This level of purpose not only maximises the impact of your money but also gives you a sense of control. You're no longer just reacting to bills and expenses; you're strategically managing your income with clarity and intent.

One of the greatest benefits of purposeful money management is the reduction in financial stress. When you know exactly where your money is going and why, you eliminate uncertainty. This frees you to invest in opportunities, plan for the unexpected and still enjoy your life, knowing your finances are solid. Purposeful planning accelerates your progress towards your goals, whether saving for a property, growing your portfolio or securing your family's future. By making this decision, you set the foundation for long-term financial security and peace of mind.

This mindset shift transforms the way you manage your money, helping you build wealth, reduce stress and stay in control of your financial future.

Decision #9. Learn to take educated risks

Creating financial success is going to require you to embrace strategic risk taking. Since you cannot avoid risk, you must learn to manage it wisely.

It can feel intimidating at first, but that's only because you're not used to flexing your risk-taking muscle. We're often taught to play it safe, but that mindset tends to leave us stuck in the middle. It's time to train that new muscle and just know you are not alone in doing it. Start by taking baby risks, learn to make effective decisions and get to growing that muscle and overcome fear.

Decision #10. Utilise leverage and debt strategically

Leverage and debt are powerful tools to accelerate your financial growth, especially in property investment, but only if used wisely.

The key is to make the decision to use debt strategically, with a clear plan for managing and eventually eliminating it.

Many investors run into trouble by taking a reactive approach—focusing only on how to buy the next asset without considering the bigger picture of wealth building. This short-sighted strategy can leave them vulnerable. The real power comes from integrating leverage into a comprehensive wealth system that guides you systematically and predictably towards financial freedom.

Decision #11. Be strategic

The typical investment strategy most would-be investors deploy is a strategy of buy and hope. Hardly a plan for financial success.

To succeed as an investor, you need more than random actions; you need a strategic, personalised plan that not only helps you move from one deal to the next, and the next, but helps you move systematically through the five phases of the wealth-creation journey.

A well-crafted strategy brings focus, ensuring every financial move is intentional and keeps you on track. It also needs to be flexible, adapting to changes in life and markets while maintaining your long-term vision.

Decision #12. Commit to paying the price

When the bill comes due for your wealth building you either pay it upfront with the investment of your time, energy and focus or you pay it later, when you have to face the reality of your financial life having not taken action.

This is where delayed gratification becomes such an important trait. We all know that building wealth doesn't happen overnight, that it requires an upfront commitment. You have to be willing to invest in getting your real-life financial education, having the courage to step outside your comfort zone, learning to take calculated risks, and implement what you have learned. This decision is about recognising that the path to financial success demands effort, time and often short-term sacrifices.

By making the decision to pay the price upfront, you are positioning yourself to reap the rewards later. It's the foundation that separates those who dream about wealth from those who achieve it.

Decision #13. Protect yourself and your wealth

Building wealth isn't only about how much you make; it's also about how much you keep. Anyone who (like me) has lost everything and had to start again knows the value of having a system to protect what you grow. This means creating a financial fortress around yourself, your family and your portfolio, giving it the resilience it needs to weather any storm.

Decision #14. Commit until you achieve the result

Remember, every master was once a beginner. No one was born an expert. True commitment means sticking with your plan through difficult times, learning from mistakes, and continuously adapting. You can hope for smooth sailing, but squalls are usually not an 'if' but a 'when'. No matter what challenges you face, far better to meet them head on and be ready to adjust, re-strategise and refocus your portfolio towards your end goal. And be sure to learn the lessons from the challenges presented to you.

Make the decision to stay the course, and success becomes inevitable.

Taking control of your financial future starts with a moment of clarity—fronting up to your finances and accepting personal responsibility for where you are and where you want to go.

These 14 decisions are the foundation for building real, lasting wealth. As we continue through this book, we will explore each decision in greater depth, giving you the tools and resources to help you follow through successfully.

Congratulations on taking ownership of your financial situation and embracing the responsibility that comes with it! You are positioning yourself not only to build wealth, but also to create a future of financial freedom and opportunity.

Every step from here is yours to take, with confidence and purpose.

Power points

- There's one thing that's riskier than investing, and that's not investing.

- These are the 14 decisions you must make to break free from the middle:

  1. Commit to becoming wealthy. Nothing moves forward until you make this decision.

  2. Focus on foundations. Building your wealth foundations means raising your *financial IQ*, setting up a *personal finance system*, turning on your *millionaire mode*, constructing your *wealth team*, building your *peer group* and setting your *strategic plan*. The stronger your foundation, the stronger your *future freedom* will be.

  3. Treat your financial life as a business. Treating your finances as a hobby gives you hobby-like results.

  4. Seek real-life financial education beyond formal systems. The formal education system will never teach you to be free; it can't. Its job is to prepare you for the job market, to join the economic wheel of society and to be a good tax-paying citizen.

  5. Build an A-team of wealth advisers with proven results. Leverage the expertise, experience and systems of others to access resources beyond your own and avoid bottlenecking your success.

  6. Qualifications do not mean qualified to help you grow your wealth. Results and experience trumps all.

  7. Learn strategically and implement effectively. Follow the rule: learn one thing, do one thing. Avoid binge

learning and focus on creating meaningful change, one step at a time.

8. Be purposeful with money. Every dollar in your life needs a plan and a purpose.

9. Learn to take educated risks. Financial success requires embracing strategic risks; since risk is unavoidable, focus on managing it wisely.

10. Utilise leverage and debt strategically. Leverage and debt can accelerate financial growth, particularly in property investment, but only when used wisely.

11. Be strategic. The buy-and-hope investment strategy doesn't work. Get a strategic plan to grow your wealth towards financial freedom.

12. Commit to paying the price. In wealth building, you either invest time, energy and focus upfront, or face the consequences later if you haven't acted.

13. Protect yourself and your wealth. Building wealth isn't only about how much you make; it's also about how much you keep.

14. Commit until you achieve the result. Every master started as a beginner. True commitment means persevering through challenges, learning from mistakes and adapting until you reach your goal. Make the decision to stay the course, and success becomes inevitable.

CHAPTER 6

FOLLOW THROUGH

In the previous chapter we finished off with the last of the 14 decisions, being all about committing until you achieve the result. Of course, this is easier said than done.

It's certainly useful in a world where we face so many seemingly urgent competing priorities in our lives. Our attention is being pulled in different directions and we have only a few tools to help us stay the course and maintain our commitment to our decisions.

The solution? One word: habit.

We'll spend more time on developing your wealth-building habits in chapter 7, but here I want to introduce what I consider to be the number one wealth-building habit that any aspiring investor can implement to change the direction of their financial life and help them break free from the financial middle.

Before I get into the specifics of this habit and introduce the tools and step-by-step guide on how to install it into your life, let's take a moment to understand why building your wealth-building habits is so important.

Our brains are wired to create shortcuts. Anything we have repeated often, and anything our subconscious mind deems to be of importance to us—whether it's a way of thinking or a specific set of action steps—our brain goes to work to streamline the activity to make it more efficient. We don't have to think about it; we go into autopilot.

In short, habits are mental shortcuts we set up so we don't have to actually make conscious decisions around common tasks.

As we know, these habits can be positive or negative. We have all had experiences of both. Positive habits uplift our lives and negative habits pull us down or keep us trapped in never-ending loops.

Our financial habits can be formed through our experiences growing up and watching what others do with money. We tend to follow the same patterns of behaviour we observe without really thinking about why we do what we do and what impact it could have on our life. I help you unpack some of these ideas when we go through the money lens exercise in chapter 7.

Unless you had a very fortunate, privileged upbringing, or perhaps had parents who were very intentional in how they participated in investing or taught you the money game, you likely formed some financial habits that are keeping you stuck right where you are.

Let me introduce you to 'the money night'. This one habit, which I have taught to thousands of investors over the years, has done more to impact people's financial results than almost anything else. Not because it is super technical or advanced—it's the complete opposite—but because it's simple and foundational, and anyone can do it.

What the money night gives you is a simple, easy-to-follow framework that will help you stay on top of your money, so you never again need to complain to yourself, 'I just don't know where my money went'.

I have prepared a money night guide for you to implement, which you can download at www.escapethemiddle.com. So what is a money night? Very simply, it's a one-hour meeting you schedule with yourself once a week with the sole purpose of helping you take care of your finances.

Let's walk through the seven simple steps to running your money night.

Step 1. Schedule it!

Decide on a day and time to hold your weekly money night, put it in your calendar on repeat so it's a regular and habitual meeting with yourself, then do anything else you need to do to make sure you follow through with it. Create reminders, set alarms, write notes — anything to ensure you follow through with your commitment until you do it often enough that it becomes a habit.

Of course, it doesn't need to be a night-time activity, but this is when most people have the time. The trick is to find a time you can commit to. My personal favourite was always Monday night, which I called 'Money Monday'. I would kick off a new week by taking care of my finances and doing something empowering for my future — a great way to win the week from day one.

Step 2. Review your personal financial goals and investments (5 mins)

Having turned up for your money night, give yourself a pat on the back for following through with your commitment. Your first step is to take five minutes to look over your financial goals, your FFF and any existing investments. This helps you to align your thinking back to your goals and commitments to yourself. If you don't have any financial goals yet, use your financial freedom figure to decide on and write down at least one mini-goal whose achievement will have a solid impact on your results. Make it both achievable and meaningful while you build your wealth-building habits. Many people make things way more complicated than they need to be. The biggest win for you right now is to begin creating the habit of being intentional with your money.

Step 3. Review your previous week's finances (10 mins)

What you're checking on right now is whether anything relating to your finances that you intended for the past week took place. Were your savings and spendings on track? Did you make your micro investments (more on this later)? Did you pay the bills and make the transfers you intended?

Take a moment to digest what you are taking stock of and plan your next steps.

Step 4. Plan your week ahead (15 mins)

What is due this week for you? Do you need to move money for better efficiency, set aside savings, pay bills, open a new account or make an investment? Get clear on what you need to accomplish and create a list of action steps. This will become more streamlined when we dive into creating your personal finance farm in Part IV.

Step 5. Automate (15 mins)

With your plan for the week in place and clarity around the micro steps you will be taking, now use technology to your advantage to make it easier. Set up automations such as direct debits, online transfers, and automatic investment or savings contributions. Let technology handle the routine tasks so you can take them off your to-do list, freeing up your time and energy to focus on other important areas of your life.

Step 6. Learn something new (15 mins)

Congratulations, you've just handled your weekly finances in 45 minutes! It may take a little longer on your first few money nights as you get familiar with the process, but once you're in the flow, it becomes easily manageable.

Remember, though, we set aside a full hour for your money night, so don't waste the last 15 minutes. Use the time to learn something new about money or wealth building. Listen to a podcast on investing, read an article or a few pages of a book, or have a meaningful conversation with your partner about finances. My wife and I speak most days about how we can grow our empire and brainstorm on the deals that come to our table. Commit to continual learning and start building your understanding of the language of money.

Consistent positive actions turn into lasting habits when you reinforce the experience with something rewarding. So take a moment to celebrate doing something great for yourself and your future. Watch a movie with your partner or open a bottle of wine (no reason your money night can't be fun)! Do whatever brings you a little joy as a way to honour the new commitments you're following through on.

Many investors I have worked with found this habit to be a game-changer. They gained more clarity, enjoyed greater control, built their confidence, made more money, reduced inefficiencies and accelerated their results.

Anyone can do it—including you!

Power points

- Our brains are wired to create shortcuts. When we repeatedly think or do something important to us, the brain streamlines it for efficiency, allowing us to shift into autopilot without conscious effort.

- Habits are mental shortcuts that free us from making conscious decisions for routine tasks. Positive habits uplift us while negative ones drag us down or trap us in endless loops.

- The most powerful wealth-building habit is scheduling a consistent 'money night'—one hour, once a week to take care of your finances. Download a money night guide at www.escapethemiddle.com. The seven steps to running your money night are:

  1. Schedule it!

  2. Review your personal financial goals and investments (5 minutes)

  3. Review your previous week's finances (10 minutes)

  4. Plan your week ahead (15 minutes)

  5. Automate (15 minutes)

  6. Learn something new (15 minutes)

  7. Celebrate!

PART III

TURN ON YOUR MILLIONAIRE MODE

CHAPTER 7

YOUR MONEY MIRROR

Do you have a dirty mind? Well, do ya? No, not like that…well maybe that, but I'm talking about a dirty money mind. And the answer is most likely *yes*.

Let's face it, most of us did not receive much of an education on how to think about money. It simply wasn't spoken about often or we were taught very disempowering things like 'money doesn't grow on trees', or 'you must have money to make money', or 'that's not for people like us', and so on. We pick up all these potentially destructive beliefs from family and friends, through social conditioning and through our own life experiences.

My experience working with thousands of investors over the years has shown me that the biggest factors differentiating those who build wealth from those who don't are mindset, attitude and their relationship with money—not how much capital they start with.

I can give you all the strategies and education, the right team, even great deals on a silver platter, but if you don't take care of the most valuable piece of real estate you own—your mind—you won't execute at the level required to achieve success. Those hidden mental blocks will keep resurfacing, leaving you stuck in a cycle of repeating the same mistakes, missing out on opportunities or procrastinating on the actions you know are crucial for your progress.

So how do you break free from this cycle? It all starts with cleaning up your mindset and reprogramming how you think about money. Think of this chapter as like looking into the financial mirror at how you think and interact with money in your life, and how to begin cleaning it up.

Let's take our first look into the mirror now and begin by identifying where you currently stand in your relationship with money by discovering which of the five money teams you're playing in. We will then shift gears and flick the switch to your millionaire mode as we unpack your personal money lens.

The five money teams

The results you're getting in life right now are a reflection of how you are playing the game. If you want to achieve different, better outcomes, you need to change the rules you're operating by. In the financial world, people typically fall into one of five teams: the Hoarders, the Gamblers, the Rookies, the Peacocks and the Investors.

The Hoarders

Picture Team Hoarders playing on a muddy field, holding on to every ball that comes their way. They cling to it, afraid to move or to lose control.

They follow conservative rules that are not necessarily bad, but they're not ideal for building wealth. Hoarders stay stuck on the field, never reaching their financial goals.

I meet many people like this. They have saved well, paid off debt, perhaps even built a financial base, but they're not free. Why? Because their money isn't working for them—it's lazy. They keep saving out of fear.

The truth is you can't save your way to wealth. If you spend all your time hoarding, you may never enjoy the game.

There used to be a regular attendee at my live events, a woman named Helen. I saw her again and again, year after year, yet nothing in her financial situation seemed to change. Helen had a solid foundation—her home was almost paid off, and she had a large amount of money sitting in the bank—but no investments. She was an incredible saver, but fear held her back. Fear of making a wrong move and losing what she'd worked so hard to save, and an even deeper fear about where she'd end up financially in the future.

As she neared 60, the weight of that fear became heavier. She was stuck in a job she didn't enjoy, exhausted from the grind, yet unable to retire because the fear of not having enough for a comfortable future kept her trapped. Helen was frozen on the field, watching her money sit in the bank earning less than 3 per cent, all while feeling life was passing her by. The fear paralysed her, and she couldn't take the next step to invest and grow her wealth.

Every year she came back to the events, hoping for something to change, but the fear always won. Then one day she stopped coming. I often wonder about Helen. Did she finally break free from the fear that held her captive? Did she take control of her future? Or is she still working in a job that drains her, her money sitting idle in the bank, slowly losing value as time passes? I truly hope she found her way, but I can't shake the concern that she may still be stuck, her dreams of a comfortable, fulfilling retirement slipping ever further away.

The Gamblers

Gamblers are out for the big plays and full-field conversions, often trying risky moves without preparation. Some are extreme, while others simply take on more risk than they should or over-leverage without protection.

They chase shiny objects and get-rich-quick schemes, neglecting the fundamentals of building a solid investment portfolio. You could almost call them gullible, as they fall for shortcuts to financial goals without putting in the work.

Gamblers are out there. They give it a crack but often operate without strategy, hoping one of their big plays will pay off. They avoid learning the essentials to understanding how wealth is built. Many lose it all but before long are on the hunt again for the next big play, trapped in a repeating cycle.

Over the years I've come across many gamblers, and it seems a lot of them are especially drawn to cryptocurrency trading schemes. There's always a 'new' and supposedly 'different' one popping up. Every six months or so I get unsolicited messages from people trying to convince me to join the latest trading bot that's supposedly delivering astronomical returns. They claim it's safe, that the creators have built billion-dollar companies before and that they're making thousands a week from it. And of course, they assure me it's not like the last one they messaged me about—or the one before that.

I've developed a keen sense for spotting scams from a mile away and my BS radar is finely tuned. I always decline politely, and without fail, about six months later, I get another message touting the 'new, even better and safer' version of the same old story.

The Rookies

The Rookies are just beginning to realise there's a game being played. They've heard about the field, the goal, and maybe even a ball somewhere, but they're still figuring out what these things look like and how they fit together.

For now, they spend their time running up and down the field—desperately tired, yet too caught up in the chaos to pause and ask, *'What's actually going on here?'*

But every player starts somewhere. With a little guidance, they might just surprise themselves. At this stage, raising their financial IQ and seeking mentorship is not just helpful—it's essential.

The Peacocks

The Peacocks are all about appearances. They show up at life's stadium in a fancy car they can barely afford, dressed in the best gear and looking like success. They talk a big game to make sure everyone notices, but underneath there's little substance.

When the ball comes their way, they drop it—too focused on looking the part rather than being the part. In the world of money, Peacocks buy flashy cars, take luxury vacations and wear designer clothes, often spending beyond their means. They're often in debt, living paycheque to paycheque, one bad turn away from gameplay destruction.

The Investors

Investors are a special team. They know the field, the rules and take time to study the game before jumping in. While they don't know everything, they understand their first steps.

Investors know how to use the ball and fully understand the end goal of the game. Over time they have developed the necessary skills. They know how to play and surround themselves with strong team players.

Investors know when to pass the ball and see the value in hiring coaches for advanced strategies and an edge over others.

However, none of this guarantees Investors won't run into trouble. Maybe a team member is not a good team player. Perhaps the field has some potholes in it.

Regardless, Investors keep honing their skills. They change strategies and adapt to various scenarios until they hit the goal. That means Investors can also step onto a bigger field to shoot for bigger goals.

Have you figured out which team you are playing in, and which team you want to be a part of? Everyone aims to be on the Investors' team, but are your actions aligned with that goal?

The good news is you can always switch teams. It starts with being honest and choosing to be strategic with your money. But switching means adopting new rules. It takes plenty of courage to make the switch and not everyone is comfortable with stepping onto a new path and leaving everything they know behind, even if it is painful to stay there.

What you already know is that you can't win the game using the default rules. Those rules are designed to keep you firmly on the field, running around like worker bees powering the economic machine.

How do you make the switch, though? Let's map out your escape from any mental traps you might be stuck in as you shift into millionaire mode.

The two key shifts to flick the switch to your millionaire mode

Here's a question for you. Which comes first: having a million dollars in your bank account or becoming a millionaire as a person, by which I mean becoming the kind of person who can create this kind of outcome to begin with?

The answer is very clearly the latter.

This is not about achieving an outcome of a million dollars. It could be any financial goal you set for yourself. It's about understanding that in order to create a new level of success in your life, you have to become a different person, a more accomplished version of yourself.

This is why we see Lotto winners who win millions of dollars but blow it all within a few short years. They came into the money by luck, but they hadn't changed, so their external results quickly rewound to match their internal operating system.

This is a core foundation of wealth building and success in any venture you deem important for yourself. If you want to raise the level of results you're achieving, you first have to raise the standards to which you are playing the game of life.

You will never out-earn yourself.

There are two key areas you need to focus on transforming to turn on what I call your 'millionaire mode'.

The first step is to shift your beliefs about money and wealth. To get new results, you need a new way of thinking. We do this through a process called 'cleaning your money lens', where we uncover the beliefs and programming around money that have shaped your current results. Then we'll transform them into an empowering wealth-building mindset to guide you towards your future goals.

The second key to unlocking your millionaire mode is to raise your standards with regard to how you approach life and to level up your habits. In the next chapter I'll introduce you to the 15 habits I've seen wealthy and successful investors practise over decades—habits that set them apart and led to different results.

Let's begin by cleaning your personal money lens.

Clean your money lens

As we go through life, we learn from those around us and our environment about how we're supposed to behave, who we're supposed to become, and what we should or shouldn't expect—all of which shapes our understanding of life. We are taught by our parents and those close to us, by the education system and by social norms. We reflect and reinforce these lessons when we become adults. In short, who we are today is not who we were born as. Rather, we are a construct of all the beliefs we have absorbed from others and the environment around us (see figure 7.1).

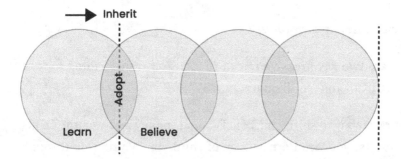

Figure 7.1: inherited belief systems

What are some of the beliefs about money that you have inherited and where did they come from?

Write down the top three you can identify. (Awareness is the first step to transformation.)

These belief systems become the lens or filter through which we interpret everything. It's not what happens to us in life, but rather the meaning we give to what happens to us that dictates our behaviour. The way we process this information shapes how we act and engage with it, leading us towards a set of habitual behaviours. What we consistently repeat eventually creates the results we experience in life (see figure 7.2).

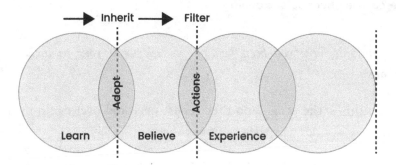

Figure 7.2: the action filter

What has been your experience of money in your life to date?

What have you habitually done that has created the results you're currently living?

Level up your standards and habits

Our results consistently reinforce our underlying belief systems and behaviour patterns, and create a set of predictable outcomes. These predictable outcomes now become our version of *reality*, and we begin living by a set of *standards* that forms a *ceiling* over what we should and should not expect in life, and this forms an aspect of our *identity* (see figure 7.3). And as human beings we do whatever we possibly can to stay consistent with who we believe we are.

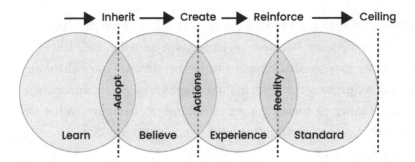

Figure 7.3: the unconscious ceiling

What standards have you been holding yourself to in your financial life to date?

For many this is the same loop they repeat over and over again in life, and they wonder why they can't get ahead.

Does this resonate with you? When I properly unpack this with investors, you see it in their eyes as the penny drops, and they go, 'Ahhh, now I know why'.

That's an empowering moment.

Have any of your own beliefs come to mind as you read this? If not, revisit the process and give yourself the gift of unravelling the beliefs that are still affecting you today.

So how do we shift these old belief systems and behaviour patterns into a more empowering mindset (see figure 7.4)? The first step is to truly decide you want more out of life and figure out what that 'more' looks like for you.

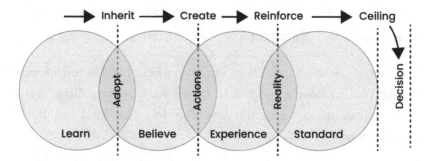

Figure 7.4: a true decision

What is the new decision you are ready to make for your financial future?

Nothing happens until a true decision is made. You may find even reading this that some of these deeper belief systems come up for you. Things like, *Isn't it greedy to want more? I should just be grateful for what I have.*

I agree about being grateful for your many blessings in life, but it isn't greedy to want more. When you say to yourself, *I want to be wealthier,* is it really about the money? Or is it about what the extra money can do for you and those around you?

Because what's wrong with wanting a better lifestyle? What's wrong with wanting to have more time to do what you love to do with the people you love, rather than what you have to do to pay the bills? What's wrong with wanting the opportunity to pursue your passions? What's wrong with having the resources to be able to fully explore this beautiful planet we have the privilege to live on? And what's wrong with wanting to create more, so you can serve more and give more?

Answer: nothing.

I'd even go so far as to say that it's selfish and lazy not to improve your financial situation. One question I have consistently asked in the live events I have run over the years is this: 'Who wants to give back to the world in a bigger way than they are currently doing?'

You should see the hands shoot up. Overwhelmingly—and I mean 99 per cent of people—say that giving back is something that's really important to them. But how can you give what you don't have yourself?

Remember, money is just a unit of choice, and you should have all the choices you want in life.

Once you have truly decided, the next step has everything to do with awareness (see figure 7.5). Actually taking the time to reflect on what in your life has brought you to the level of results you are currently experiencing in life.

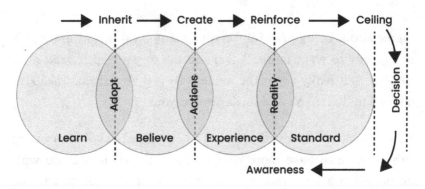

Figure 7.5: bring the unconscious into the conscious

What actions have you consistently taken?

What beliefs have you adopted as your own?

Where in your life have you just followed the status quo of everyone else?

and

Why are you where you are in your financial life?

What we're doing here is uncovering our habitual thought patterns and actions, taking them from the unconscious 'autopilot' mode we spend a lot of our time in and bringing them into our conscious decision-making mind so we can re-choose our experience.

When you have the opportunity to re-choose your experience and actions, you can now ask these very empowering questions:

Who do I need to become now in order to create this new level of result in my life?

and

What new ways of thinking and doing do I need to adopt?

Asking yourself these types of questions opens a new opportunity to tap into resources you already have within you.

I understand it's easy to pose these questions to yourself and to write down some very inspiring and practical answers. Ultimately, it's putting them into practice that will dictate your results. Stay with me and work this through for yourself here and now—your future self will thank you for your commitment, I guarantee it.

Changing often long-held belief systems and behaviour patterns can be tough. After all, you likely have been running this habitual mode of thinking, doing and being for decades and your unconscious mind will fight to maintain this well-worn groove of neural pathways it has developed. It's time to close off that path and flick the switch into your millionaire mode way of thinking. To do this, you have to train your mind into a new way of being as you level up your own identity (see figure 7.6, overleaf). This begins by installing a new set of strategic habits designed to deliver a very different level of performance. These habits aren't about drastic, one-time actions but rather, small, intentional changes that, when practised consistently, build momentum over time.

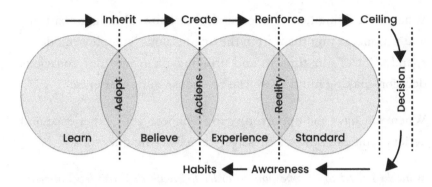

Figure 7.6: levelling up your habits

We'll spend a lot more time on habits in the next chapter; however, here are some interesting questions to get you started as you work your way through your money lens:

What habits have been serving you in your financial life?

What habits have been keeping you stuck where you are in your financial life?

What habits do you feel have been sabotaging your success?

Your beliefs and habits can lift you to new levels of success in life or they can be your hidden saboteurs, lurking in the background and thwarting your attempts at breaking free from the status quo. Now is the time to decide on a new set of habits aligned with the new standards you have set for your life.

As you repeat these habits consistently, the effort eases when what once was new to you becomes a part of your new identity as the millionaire mode version of you and a new set of neural pathways is ingrained (see figure 7.7).

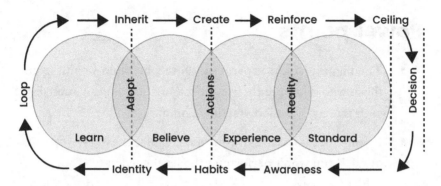

Figure 7.7: your millionaire identity

This new version of you—with greater self-awareness and playing life at a higher level than you were before—will learn new things, adopt new beliefs, take different actions, and around the money lens loop you go as you continue to level up your life. You can watch a training video and download a workbook for this at www .escapethemiddle.com.

It may have occurred to you that the money lens framework could readily be applied outside of the wealth-building context. It could be used, for example, wherever you seek to 'upgrade' key areas of your life including relationships, health, careers and family relations. So once you're done here, why not choose another area in which to rewrite your stories … until you are levelling up all areas of your life.

Now, time to talk habits.

Power points

- The biggest factors separating those who build wealth from those who don't are their mindset, attitude and relationship with money, not their starting capital.

- If you don't take care of your most valuable asset—your mind—you won't perform at the level needed to achieve success.

- The results you're experiencing now reflect how you're playing the game. To achieve better outcomes, you need to change the rules you're following.

- In the financial world, people generally fall into one of five teams:

  1. **Hoarders** are great savers, but their money isn't working for them.

  2. **Gamblers** are always out for the big plays and get rich quick.

  3. **Rookies** are just starting out, running hard but unsure of their next play.

  4. **Peacocks** may look the part but they're only playing.

  5. **Investors** strategically learn the rules of the game and grow their portfolios.

- You can't win the game playing by society's default rules.

- What comes first: having a million dollars in your account, or becoming the kind of person who can create and sustain that level of wealth in the first place?

- There are two key areas you need to focus on transforming to switch on your *millionaire mode*: rewiring your beliefs about money and wealth, and raising your standards and upgrading your habits accordingly.

- The money lens exercise helps you uncover your underlying beliefs and programming about money and wealth building, guiding you to elevate your mindset and habits for a new financial reality.

- Our beliefs are often not our own; we inherit them from those around us.

- Our belief systems act as the lens or filter through which we interpret everything.

- The way we process information and the meaning we assign to it shape our actions, driving us towards habitual behaviours.

- Our habitual behaviours eventually create the results we experience in life.

- The results we consistently experience reinforce our core beliefs and behaviour patterns, creating a cycle of predictable outcomes we come to expect in life.

- These predictable outcomes shape our reality, setting a ceiling on what we believe we should expect in life and forming a key part of our identity.

- We do what we can to stay consistent with who we believe we are.

CHAPTER 8

THE 15 HABITS OF MILLIONAIRE INVESTORS

It's estimated that over 40 per cent of our life is governed by unconscious habits, meaning nearly half of what we do happens on autopilot—without intentional design.

Our brain naturally forms patterns, creating neural pathways that shift actions from conscious choices to unconscious routines, repeating the same patterns day in and day out in order to make what we do more efficient. But what if our ways of thinking and doing are not tuned to high performance?

Consider this: You jump in your car on your way to work or to a place you frequent often. You have lots of things on your mind, yet somehow you wind up exactly where you intended to go, and you ask yourself, *How did I do that?*

So what happened in that moment? Your autopilot flicked on. Your unconscious knew where you were headed; your mind and body knew how to drive the car and did so without your thinking twice about it. Your conscious mind was busy elsewhere while you were drinking a coffee, listening to music, checking your mirrors, stopping at lights and a host of other actions as your autopilot got you to your destination.

Many times I've found that my autopilot flicked off only when I pulled into the car park at my destination, leaving me wondering how on earth I actually got there. At this point you may be thinking that you don't want to be on the road at the same time as me.

Maybe this is not a thing for you, but something similar has happened to you in another arena of life? Autopilot mode may kick in at work, in your relationship, with your kids or when you get home from work. I wonder what your financial autopilot does with your money and finances?

Our aim is to get out of our old autopilot mode and begin being very intentional and conscious about the new habits we're choosing to introduce into our lives, habits that can generate very different outcomes for us.

This system works well if those autopilot habits are deliberately shaped to move you towards your goals. Unfortunately, for most people these habits are a mix of inherited traits, emotional reactions, social expectations and random triggers.

After working for decades with thousands of successful individuals I have learned that wealth and success are not about grand, one-off actions; rather, they're built through small, consistent, daily actions. These actions accumulate over time, eventually snowballing into what we call wealth and success. In short, wealth is a habit.

The habit of wealth

The first step to transforming a habit is awareness. Once you observe it, you can choose to change it. Having studied successful people for more than 20 years, I have identified key habits that most, if not all, wealthy individuals share.

As you start introducing these new habits and shifting into a more intentional way of living, you may be wondering what are some of the specific habits you can adopt that will help transform your thinking and elevate your life to the next level.

Are you ready to take control, switch off your autopilot and activate your millionaire mindset? Let's dive in.

Habit #1. They challenge their comfort zones

As humans, we crave comfort and certainty around what comes next. That comfort zone can quickly become a prison, however. Little changes within it, and life can become a repetitive cycle (see figure 8.1). If you're content, that's fine, but if you're seeking new results, you are likely disappointed.

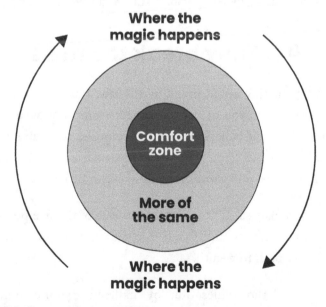

Figure 8.1: the comfort zone trap

Perhaps you're one of those brave souls who are tired of the status quo and ready to break free. You start to push towards the edge of your comfort zone, where change happens, but as you get closer your nerves kick in and your stress mounts. Eventually it becomes overwhelming, and you retreat to the perceived safety of your comfort zone—only to feel that familiar discontent creep back in again later.

Sound familiar?

The most successful people regularly challenge their comfort zones. But it doesn't require taking wild leaps; it's about making small, strategic changes over time.

Success is a marathon, not a sprint.

One practical habit I have shared with my clients is scheduling a 'do something different day'. Purposefully shake up your routine: try a new restaurant, take a different route home or engage in a new conversation. This simple practice helps you build the muscle to step outside your comfort zone, especially when your results and wealth depend on it.

Habit #2. They break the rules

Here I'm not talking about breaking the law. Rather, I'm referring to rules imposed on you by others, expectations of how you should behave to meet their beliefs or even self-imposed rules about what's possible. These rules often come from those closest to us, including family and friends, and those expectations can be heavy.

Jim Rohn famously said, 'You are the average of the five people you spend the most time with.' If your circle is positive, great. If not, it can limit your path to wealth.

It's okay to break those rules. Start by challenging your own limiting beliefs, and it will become easier to break the expectations others place on you. Focus on what's keeping you stuck, especially rules and conventions that prevent you from dreaming big.

Habit #3. They take total responsibility

Millionaire investors understand they are in control of shaping their lives and they take full responsibility for how their life turns out. If you're not succeeding, the issue might not be external—it could be you. It's easy to fall into a victim mindset and blame others or external events, but that won't change your results. You have to take responsibility for where you are, who you are and whatever results you're getting, and then decide to do something about it.

You will face challenges in life—everyone does. It's your response to these challenges that truly matters. Wealth creation isn't smooth sailing; there will always be squalls along the way. What sets successful people apart is their willingness to navigate those obstacles and keep moving forward.

Taking responsibility for where you are and the actions you take gives you control over your future. Millionaire investors own their choices, learn from setbacks and focus on the next steps. In the end, responsibility is the key to reclaiming your power and determining your success.

Make the decision that no matter what happens in the future, you will take responsibility for where you are and do something about it.

Habit #4. They focus on their strengths

Wealthy people prioritise leveraging their strengths rather than trying to fix their weaknesses. Their expertise is often narrow but deep, which allows them to create immense value. This is where they thrive, where they are in flow and where they can make their biggest impact. By maximising this value differential, they generate their highest income and build wealth.

I guide many of my clients through a process to uncover their 'wealth genius', helping them identify their greatest strengths, manage their weaknesses so they don't hinder progress, commit to mastering key areas and build a supportive team. This approach allows them to achieve far more than they could alone, and it is a heck of a lot more fun.

When your wealth-building strategy aligns with your strengths, it becomes a path of flow rather than struggle. It goes far beyond just your investment strategy, positively impacting your business, relationships and decision making. As Peter Drucker said, 'A person can perform only from strength. One cannot build performance on weakness.'

Habit #5. They have daily rituals that set them up for success

Every successful person I know has a strategic daily routine that sets them up for success. These routines—ranging from exercise to meditation, time with loved ones, reading, goal-setting and more—are not random. They're refined over years or modelled on other successful people.

One of my key daily rituals is what I call 'clouds and dirt'. I spend time with my head in the clouds, zooming out from the day-to-day to review my goals, visualising my future and thinking creatively. Then I ground myself, with my feet in the dirt, focusing on action and getting things done. It's important to dream, but also to act.

Finally, I find time in between for silent meditation to clear my mind and connect with myself.

These practices don't need to take much time but they can create ripples across all areas of your life. Consider what daily rituals, small but impactful, could help you in areas such as success, wealth, health, family and fulfillment. Keep them simple and easy to maintain, and watch the difference they make.

Habit #6. They model success

There are two main ways to learn in life. The first—whether you're tying your shoes, riding a bike or making investments—is by trial and error. But the 'error' part can be costly in terms of time, money and sleepless nights. If you have ever made a mistake investing, you know it's often not a cheap experience.

The second way is through modelling success. Find someone who has achieved the results you want, study how they did it and copy them. In school, copying may be called cheating; in life it's a fast track to success. Learning what to do—and, equally important, what *not* to do—can be your shortcut. By tapping into proven systems that deliver predictable results, you can save yourself a lot of headaches.

Personally, I've had mentors in every area of my life, from investing and business to relationships, spiritual teachers and personal growth. These extraordinary people have shared their wisdom with me, and I can say with certainty I wouldn't be where I am without their guidance. Now I have the privilege of paying it forward and guiding others on their journey to success.

Most people spend their lives waiting for 'permission' to go after what they want. It's like they're looking for a universal sign, waiting for all the stars to align, for a guardian angel to give them the go-ahead. But guess what? Those signs may never come, or they may go unnoticed or be ignored out of fear.

Many unconsciously seek approval—from parents, partners, friends or bosses—more than they seek results. People are drawn to familiarity, and stepping outside your comfort zone can make others uncomfortable too, because it forces them to reflect on their own lives, which can be unsettling.

The wealthy and successful, on the other hand, don't wait for permission. They don't mind standing out or going against the grain. Their permission comes from within, aligned with their values, priorities and outcomes. As a result, they take swift action, and their results follow much faster.

Habit #7. They prioritise and protect their time

The wealthy understand that time is their most valuable resource and they protect it fiercely. Time wasters stand no chance with them. At any given moment, we are limited by various resources—money, knowledge, energy and, most crucially, time. Time is the true currency of wealth, and unlike other factors it is the one constant for all of humanity. Regardless of background or circumstances, everyone has the same 24 hours each day to create something for their future.

The difference lies in how we use that time. Successful people don't have more time than others, but they have mastered how to prioritise it. In a world that's busier and more distracting than ever, many blame their lack of progress on a supposed shortage of time. But for most it's not a time issue; it's a priority problem. There's always time for what matters most, but only if you consciously protect it from distractions, time wasters and tasks of less importance.

Instead of focusing solely on time management, the wealthy focus on mastering their priorities. Saying no to unimportant things is just as critical as saying yes to what truly matters. Ask yourself, if you could do just one thing today to have the greatest impact on your success, what would that be? Then ask, what would be the next most important thing? By focusing on these key priorities daily, you can watch your results soar.

Imagine narrowing down your life's core areas into a list of 10 top priorities or perhaps even fewer—strategically designed to maximise your success, health, happiness and relationships. Mastering time and priorities in this way isn't just a good idea; it's the key to building lasting success.

Habit #8. They are decision-making monsters

Millionaire investors are decisive. While others hesitate over even the smallest choices, successful people make decisions swiftly and act on them. Becoming a decision-making monster involves three key steps:

1. Get clear on where you are and where you want to go.
   This clarity helps you take focused steps to bridge the gap efficiently.
2. Align your decisions with your values and goals. Always ask, 'Will this decision take me closer to my highest outcomes?' If the answer is yes, take action. If the answer is no, you already know what to do.

3. Continually level up your knowledge. The better informed you are, the better decisions you will make. And when you are unsure, tap into the experience of those who have already achieved success.

Habit #9. They are the CEO of their financial life

Most people don't approach their finances like a business, but millionaire investors do. Managing your financial life is no different from running a company—you are in the business of making investments to gain freedom and improve your life.

To succeed, adopt the mindset of a CEO overseeing your financial portfolio. Millionaire investors have made this shift, and so should you.

Ask yourself, *If I was a business, would I invest in myself?* If your answer is no, it's time to focus on the areas holding you back and start managing your financial life like a business.

Habit #10. They focus on earning

Investable income is the money available to invest after covering your living expenses, and it's a key driver of wealth and freedom.

Wealthy individuals tend to be earners who master specific skills and know how to monetise them, creating significant income by adding immense value. They also diversify, building multiple income streams. Research suggests the average millionaire has around seven income sources, but I advise my clients to focus on growing three in the next 12 months.

Start by maximising your primary income source; often the biggest opportunity is right in front of you. This is the leverage principle in action.

For those not in their dream job, consider building a side hustle to monetise a passion. These first two income streams are 'active', requiring your time and effort to grow.

The third income stream should focus on something more passive, like property investment, business ventures or lending as seed capital. The sooner you start, the quicker you will move towards financial freedom. Relying on just one income stream is highly risky.

Habit #11. They leverage like crazy

Leverage is a key principle that separates those who build wealth from those who don't. If you rely solely on your own efforts and resources, your results will always be limited. Mastering leverage means multiplying your efforts to achieve greater outcomes—because you can't reach major goals just by trading time for money.

There are six types of leverage that are like levers you can pull in areas of your life to alleviate constraints and accelerate your returns:

1. **Strengths.** You are your greatest asset. Learn to amplify and focus your strengths on your highest outcomes rather than trying to fix weaknesses and being a jack of all trades.
2. **Knowledge.** Leverage the knowledge of other people with more experience and expertise and shortcut your learning cycle instead of attempting to trial and error your way to success.
3. **People.** Build a team around you to get more done in less time, allowing you to focus on your highest value activities.

4. **Financial.** A potent wealth-building tool when used strategically and safely, allowing investors to leverage into assets beyond the cash value in their own back pocket.

5. **Network.** Investing in relationships and growing a network can bring a gold mine of introductions, valuable deals and opportunities. Though requiring time and effort, the leverage gained from a thriving network is exponential and enduring.

6. **Systems.** Don't reinvent the wheel; leverage the proven processes and technology of others. Systems are the secret sauce to getting more done with less effort.

Stop being the bottleneck to your own success and tap into resources well beyond your own. The six levers of leverage are your key to unlocking exponential results.

Habit #12. They practise delayed gratification daily

Wealth isn't built overnight. There's no quick fix or magic formula that will solve your financial problems instantly, and chasing one can be dangerous. This 'shiny object syndrome', which we discussed earlier, will kill your progress and dreams.

It's easy to see why people fall into this trap. Quick results with little effort sounds appealing, but long-term success isn't achieved through short-term decisions. Wealthy and successful individuals understand this and consistently practise delayed gratification, keeping a long-term perspective.

While it's possible to achieve great short-term results, especially with the right strategy, team and deal flow, your decisions should always align with your long-term wealth-building plan, not just what feels good in the moment.

Building wealth involves an educational cost, but the cost of ignorance is far higher. Mistakes in business and investing often cost thousands, if not more, and lead to lost time and missed opportunities.

The key lesson: Make decisions based on your long-term vision and goals, not short-term emotional impulses.

Habit #13. They are master implementers

Learning is one thing; implementation is everything. All the most beautiful and well-thought-through plans mean squat unless you do something with them.

The wealthy are master implementers—they act where others only think. I teach my clients a simple rule: 'Learn one thing, do one thing.' Whenever you learn a new tool or skill, take immediate action on it before moving on to the next lesson.

I get it, it can be fun learning, and it's easy to become a seminar junkie—I know, I've been one. I attended event after event and loved being in that environment, learning new things and sharpening my mind. Then I realised I wasn't implementing even half of what I was learning, and I had to change my philosophy if I wanted to make meaningful progress.

Habit #14: They adapt to the landscape

Millionaire investors are masters at surveying the investment landscape and adapting their approach to stay ahead. They understand that markets, economies and industries are constantly evolving, and sticking to a rigid strategy can be detrimental. Instead of following a one-size-fits-all plan, they remain flexible and ready to adjust their tactics when necessary.

These investors keep a close eye on trends, shifts and emerging opportunities. They don't just react—they anticipate. By staying informed and maintaining a broad perspective, they position themselves to make smart moves in response to changes, whether it's pivoting to a new asset class, adjusting their portfolio in light of economic shifts or seizing an opportunity others might not even recognise.

The key to their success is a willingness to adapt without losing sight of their long-term goals. They don't abandon their core strategies but rather refine them, using new information to fine-tune their decisions. This adaptability allows them to thrive in any environment, while others may struggle when market conditions change.

Habit #15. They commit to constant strategic upgrading

I'm a big advocate of having a strategic growth plan for your life. Ask yourself the question, *Who do I need to become in order to create the level of results I want in my life?* Get to work on crafting a strategic growth plan to become the kind of person who can deliver that outcome—and be ready to watch your results soar. This could be in the world of money and wealth building, in business skills or in personal transformation.

I'm not saying you should *not* learn broadly if that is something you love to do. But focusing on learning that does not serve your purpose becomes a filler activity: it occupies space and time and takes you away from more intentional growth.

If you commit to intentional mastery, you become unstoppable.

So which of these 15 habits of millionaire investors are you going to focus on implementing first? Try to do them all at once and you'll end up spinning your wheels and going nowhere fast. Instead, focus on choosing one to three habits to start and commit to massive execution and implementation, then slowly add more as you go along.

Remember, wealth creation and success in any endeavour is a marathon, not a sprint.

In any endeavour, whether its wealth creation, your health or your relationships, success is a habit. It's not about the one big thing you do that makes all the difference; rather, it's about the small, seemingly insignificant things you do on a consistent basis that stack up and up until they avalanche over into this thing called wealth and success.

The beautiful thing is that knowing wealth is a habit means you can create it too. There's nothing standing in your way. There's only you and your willingness to commit to live by a new set of standards.

Power points

- An estimated 40 per cent of our actions are driven by unconscious habits, meaning nearly half of them occur on autopilot. Successful investors adopt these positive habits:

  - Habit #1: **They challenge their comfort zones.** They challenge their comfort zones by making small, intentional changes, helping them break routines and embrace discomfort to achieve growth and wealth.

  - Habit #2: **They break the rules.** They challenge limiting beliefs and societal expectations, breaking free from conventions to unlock their potential.

  - Habit #3: **They take total responsibility.** They take full ownership of their life outcomes, recognising that their choices and actions shape their future.

  - Habit #4: **They focus on their strengths.** They leverage their strengths to create value, focusing on areas where they excel to maximise impact and results.

  - Habit #5: **They have daily rituals that set them up for success.** They establish consistent daily routines that align with their goals and create momentum for long-term success.

  - Habit #6: **They model success.** They study and emulate those who have achieved the results they desire, using proven strategies as shortcuts to success.

  - Habit #7: **They prioritise and protect their time.** They fiercely protect their time by focusing on high-impact activities and avoiding distractions.

- Habit #8: **They are decision-making monsters.** They make swift, informed decisions aligned with their goals and values to maintain momentum.

- Habit #9: **They are the CEO of their financial life.** They manage their financial life like a business, taking control of their investments and strategies for financial freedom.

- Habit #10: **They focus on earning.** They prioritise increasing their income by mastering their skills and creating multiple income streams.

- Habit #11: **They leverage like crazy.** They maximise their results by leveraging their strengths, knowledge, people, finances, networks and systems—the six levers:

  1. **Strengths.** Focus on amplifying your strengths rather than fixing weaknesses for maximum impact.

  2. **Knowledge.** Leverage others' expertise to shortcut your learning and avoid trial and error.

  3. **People.** Build a team to accomplish more in less time, allowing focus on high-value tasks.

  4. **Finances.** Apply financial leverage strategically to access assets beyond your own capital.

  5. **Network.** Grow and invest in your network to unlock valuable opportunities and introductions.

  6. **Systems.** Use proven systems and processes to accomplish more with less effort.

Stop being the bottleneck and use these six levers to unlock exponential success.

- Habit #12: **They practise delayed gratification daily.** They prioritise long-term wealth building over short-term impulses, making decisions that align with their future goals.

- Habit #13: **They are master implementers.** They focus on taking immediate action on what they learn, understanding that implementation (not just acquiring knowledge) is the key to progress.

- Habit #14: **They adapt to the landscape.** They continuously adapt their strategies to evolving market conditions while keeping their long-term goals in sight.

- Habit #15: **They commit to constant strategic upgrading.** They focus on continuous growth, crafting strategic plans to become the kind of person who achieves exceptional results.

- Wealth creation is a habit, which means it is possible for you too.

CHAPTER 9

RAISING YOUR FINANCIAL IQ

We spend most of our life working for money, yet we are never taught how to use it, manage it or grow it. Does that sound like a problem to you?

Instead, we are taught how to become worker bees—tiny cogs in the economic machine, which relies on good boys and girls who do what they are told and pay their taxes.

Screw that. You have learned the language taught to you by the system; now you must learn the language of money.

Whaddya know?

As illustrated in figure 9.1 (overleaf), there are three types of knowledge in the world.

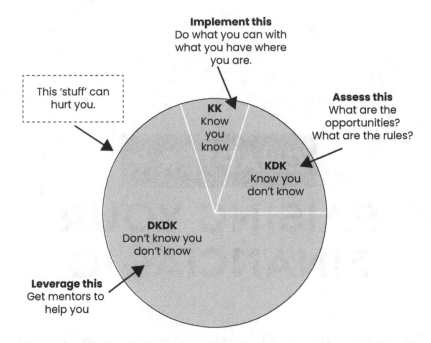

Figure 9.1: three types of knowledge

Stuff you know you know (KYK)

This is the information you're already confident in, but the key here is implementation. It's not enough simply to possess knowledge—you need to put it into action. Millionaire investors excel because they don't just sit on what they know; they actively use it to make strategic decisions and drive results. Focus on consistently applying what you know to ensure it translates into real-world progress and outcomes.

Stuff you know you don't know (KDK)

Identify the gaps in your knowledge and ask yourself what's most important to learn right now. Focus on understanding the areas that can either help you accelerate your results or prevent you from making costly mistakes.

Stuff you don't know you don't know (DKDK)

These blind spots can pose the greatest risks or present the most significant opportunities. The challenge here is that you can't actively seek out information you don't realise you need. To uncover these gaps, surround yourself with experts, mentors, and a strong network who can point out what you're missing

Some people pretend money isn't important, yet try operating effectively without it in modern society. Unless, of course, you choose to live off grid, growing your own food and being completely self-sufficient—which I'm a big fan of, by the way.

For most of us, however, money is an integral part of our daily life and I would go as far to say that getting a financial education is one of the most important forms of education you can get in life. It's the key to your becoming empowered with your money and in control of your financial future.

Learning the language of money

Visiting a foreign country where you don't know the language can feel daunting, even overwhelming, at first. You're trying to listen to what people are saying, hoping to pick up a sense of what is being communicated, but right now it just sounds like a whole lot of noise.

You begin to learn a few key words: *hello, yes, no, please, thank you, food, water, how much?* Words to help you get by. Little by little you add more words, and soon enough you are forming full sentences.

Now your rate of learning goes up dramatically, because you can interact at a deeper level. As you continue learning, more of the nuances and phrasing become apparent, and as your vocabulary expands you begin learning about the local culture and again your immersion and comprehension deepens.

Learning the language of money is no different. At first it can feel daunting, but, word by word and sentence by sentence, you begin to become more fluent. When you start to grasp the foundations of the language—from certain sounds to word and sentence structures—you have a platform to build on.

Investors who work with me are continually shocked at the level of conversations they are having after their first 12 months, compared with when they began.

Unfortunately, many people give up when things seem too complex to begin with, which is the worst mistake you can make. Remember, if nothing changes in your life, then nothing changes.

So start small, build up slowly, be gentle on yourself, and keep turning up to learn the fundamentals so your financial vocabulary and comprehension can grow, little by little.

Your river of wealth and the three key areas of financial learning

In learning the language of money and raising your financial IQ, you will discover there are three key areas to focus on. I'll explain each of them using a concept I call your 'river of wealth'.

You see, everyone has a river of wealth in their lives. The question is whether yours is a trickling stream or a raging torrent. Or is it more like a dry, barren riverbed where it feels like nothing can survive. Wherever it is right now, the river is there waiting for you to realise its potential.

All rivers begin at their source and are fed by other tributaries, increasing the volume of water. Your other income streams are like the tributaries feeding your river of wealth.

Most people have only one income stream, being their job, while other tributaries are blocked off or not flowing at all. Because most people are so financially inefficient, even this main income stream leaks out of the riverbanks and evaporates before much of it, if any at all, even reaches their river. This results in your needing to head back to the source and pump more water in with your work. We'll be plugging these leaks in Part IV.

You need to understand, though, that one of the greatest accelerators of your investment portfolio is increasing your earning potential, and the first level of education.

Learn how to earn

When I work with clients on growing their income, we first go to work on leveraging and maximising their main income stream, usually from a job or business. This is the first and main channel of their river of wealth.

There are many ways to do this, but waiting until your boss gives you the next raise or the government raises the minimum wage is not one of them. This is a middle way of increasing your income and is slow, passive and ineffective.

I take my clients through a system called the 'income freedom formula'. After we set the plan to grow the main channel of the river and increase the flow, we begin to open up the tributaries by multiplying your income streams to increase your cashflow, while diversifying and protecting your income. For me, one income stream is risky; two income streams is okay; three income streams affords stability, and over and above that you move into the realm of abundance.

When you learn how to rapidly increase your main source of income then understand how to expand your number of income streams, you not only de-risk your situation, but you tap into greater cashflow to accelerate your financial goals. As with everything else I speak about in this book, there are strategies and systems for you to do each of these.

As you begin to have some cashflow hit your river, you need to understand how to multiply it. This is where your second type of education comes into play.

Learn how to grow what you earn

If you don't get your money working hard for you, then you will spend your entire life working hard for money and stay trapped in the middle.

The key is to systematically build a portfolio of quality assets that grow your wealth and eventually provide sustainable cashflow. Keeping your cash in the bank won't get you far. It earns next to nothing, making it 'lazy money', one of my pet hates.

You'll also never save your way to wealth. You must learn to invest, turning your cashflow into assets that serve the right strategic purpose in your portfolio, then watch that river widen and deepen all the way to your financial freedom, which brings us to your third type of education.

Learn how to keep what you grow

We're not looking for flash-in-the-pan wealth; we're looking for sustainable wealth that delivers a predictable income stream you can rely on to support your chosen lifestyle.

This is where you have to learn how to protect your river—by which I mean yourself, your family and your portfolio—to secure your financial future.

This is not only about shoring up the riverbanks; it's also about ensuring you have structured your portfolio correctly, you are protecting your tributaries and assets and making sure you are not contaminating your river with the wrong things at the wrong times.

You may be wondering how you go about doing all this. As you continue this book we will be completing each step. Raising your financial IQ, at its core, means becoming a better financial decision maker.

Becoming a better financial decision maker

As I have said before and as bears repeating often, your future success depends on the strength and depth of the foundation you build at the start, and this comes back to making intelligent and thoughtful decisions along the way. The quality of your life is based on the quality of your decisions, so you must look to increasing the quality of your financial decision making.

The decision-making matrix

I'll now lay out a three-part decision-making framework through which you can filter your decisions in order to make better-quality decisions (see figure 9.2, overleaf).

**How do you feel
about this decision?**

- Is this opportunity aligned
  with my values?
- Is this opportunity aligned
  with the outcomes of my
  strategy?

**What changes might unfold in
my life if I were to make and act
upon this decision compared to
choosing the alternate option?**

- What are the costs if I
  made this decision?
  (Think financial, time, 2nd
  and 3rd order effects,
  energy).
- By making this decision,
  what other opportunities
  am I unable to take or
  execute on?

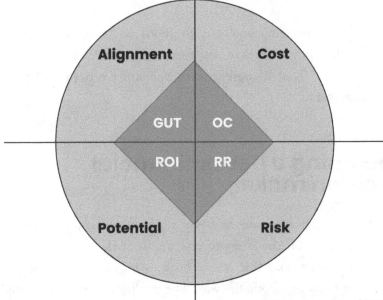

Is it worth it?

- What is the potential
  return on investment
  (ROI) of this decision?
  (Think financial, time, 2nd
  and 3rd order effects,
  energy)

**Am I comfortable with the
potential risks based on the
return I can potentially make?**

- What are the potential
  risks of the decision I am
  about to make?

Figure 9.2: the decision-making matrix

Filter #1. Alignment

I'm a big believer in making values-based financial decisions that are aligned to your highest outcomes. On the flip side, making decisions or investments that violate your values is a big no in my book. This is why being clear on your values, what and why they are important to you, and what you want your life to be about is so critical.

Let me tell you about Sarah. When I first met her she had just been through a rough divorce. Although her business was doing okay, it wasn't performing at the level Sarah wanted.

Money was tight, but she was happy in her own way. She was living in a great apartment in one of the capital cities. It was a gorgeous place overlooking a beautiful park, within walking distance of her yoga studio and her business. Life felt easy and Sarah was feeling productive and safe there, with everything at her fingertips.

The one thing she wanted to change was her financial situation. Her current lifestyle was slightly outside her budget, but rather than focusing on how to increase her income, her focus was all about reducing expenses.

At some point she talked to someone who presented themselves as having a bunch of knowledge about money and investing. They advised Sarah to move out of that apartment and effectively cut her rent in half.

From a numbers perspective, it made perfect sense, and the decision was made. But here's what happened.

Initially, Sarah had a blast moving into a new place and sharing it with two other young women. It didn't take long for the initial novelty to wear off, though.

She didn't feel inspired. She missed the convenience, comfort and privacy of her old apartment. How she felt in her old place, with nature right outside her window rather than looking out at a bare wooden fence, the feeling of having her own space set up just the way she liked it—this might not matter to everyone, but it mattered to her.

Not only was she unhappy, but her productivity also suffered, as did her income and creativity and the opportunity cost of living in a place that made Sarah unhappy turned out to be high. This is where you have to ask if saving $200 a week was worth it?

I'm not saying you should overspend or put yourself in financial stress. Be smart. The point here is that life isn't one-dimensional, and our financial decisions shouldn't be either.

You need to get into the habit of asking yourself how your decisions will impact other areas of your life and income? And to understand what the true cost of these decisions can be outside of just money.

Your environment is one of the most important investments you can make. When you're in a space that makes you feel happy, energised, inspired and productive, your ability to create and achieve more increases dramatically. Personally, I've always made it a priority to invest in my surroundings. Being in a place that encourages bigger thinking, boosts my flow, enhances creativity and provides clarity has given me an incredible return on investment.

Filter #2. Highest outcomes

Your decisions should be aligned with your highest outcomes. Get into the habit of asking yourself this very question: *Does this pathway take me closer to or further away from my highest outcomes?*

It acts as your own GPS, and can give you a clear indication of what you choose to say yes and no to in life. Both are equally important. If you are open, you will find that there is never a scarcity of opportunity or doors to walk through, but walking through the wrong door can create a distraction that costs you time, money and opportunities.

If you have completed the financial freedom exercise in chapter 4, you should have a better understanding of the outcomes you want to create.

Let me share with you a really common question I field, which may help to explain this better. People in their twenties and thirties often ask whether I feel contributing extra into a retirement account at their age is a good thing or not. It's a fair question, as this advice is commonly dispensed by family members, financial planners and accountants.

Here's how I think about it. I'm not saying it's right or the only way to do things—it's just my perspective. I'm not a big believer in retirement. I believe in setting up a life you don't need to retire from. It was always important to me to create financial freedom well before a 'supposed' retirement age, and I know I'm not alone in this.

As I write this, I'm 41 years old and superannuation in Australia is really only accessible at age 65, and that so-called retirement age is tipped to rise. So to me this retirement structure would be a 20- to 30-year strategy. There's certainly nothing wrong with having a long-term plan—in fact, I insist on it. The question is, what kind of plan do you want?

From my highest outcome perspective, this would mean putting money away for 20 to 30 years in an inflexible system that I don't control, don't get to make decisions about and don't necessarily trust won't be restricted in the future. If I run it through the decision-making filter, this would not be a place I would allocate much if any of my extra capital.

So it's a no for me. I prefer to build wealth in my own way with the flexibility I want. But hey, perhaps that's only true for me. The middle teaches us that retirement schemes are essential for future financial security, yet often they are failing people badly even with the supposed tax savings and security they propose to provide.

Of course, people closer to retirement may find a retirement fund a far bigger part of their current investment cycle. With the right timing, contribution and conditions, it could move them closer to their highest outcomes. But fair warning, the goal posts are always moving and there's nothing stopping governments from changing the rules on a whim, as it has in the past, and often not in favour of your having more choice and control.

Here's the key: get clear on your goal and make the decisions that best move you towards it.

Filter #3. The risk/reward ratio

There is risk in any investment you make. Things can always go wrong, no doubt about it. The share market or crypto markets can crash, the property market may pull back, business investments go sour.

Changes in the economy and interest rates could change your repayments. Unruly tenants could trash your property. Body corporates can make idiotic decisions. Councils can choose to change policies. In one way or another we are at the mercy of events beyond our control, both locally and globally.

As an investor, learning how to make decisions with measured risk is essential. This is where a lot of people freeze, though. They become fearful about taking any risk and wind up doing nothing, which incidentally is extremely risky in itself, as your results never change.

This is where, as an investor, we have to be able to understand our *risk/reward ratio* and become comfortable with measured risk.

You might find investing in good-quality blue chip real estate in solid locations to be a measured risk. Of course, the potential returns may not be as high as other strategies, but if you have chosen the right property as part of an effective strategy, and have done your cashflow numbers to ensure you can afford to hold it, the potential for things to go drastically wrong can be much lower.

In contrast, buying in a tiny regional town or a mining town might yield a very different risk/reward ratio. You could have a colossal return on investment if things go well. However, if something happens in the mining sector or in the economy, then you might find yourself holding an asset in a plummeting market.

I met one couple in the midst of one of the mining booms in Australia. They owned multiple properties in two specific mining towns and were achieving astronomical rents, to the point they had created what they thought was financial freedom within a few short years, earning $150k per annum in positive cashflow.

At one point they came to me for some advice about their portfolio, and after looking at everything I advised them to sell down some of their properties and migrate their money into better-quality properties in more stable areas to de-risk and stabilise their portfolio. Unfortunately, the cashflow they were enjoying was too intoxicating for them so they ignored the advice and went on their merry way.

Years later I heard from them again. Their elation had long since faded. The mining boom had ended, the rents were gone, the market had dropped by 70 to 90 per cent in the areas they had bought in, their debt levels were drastically higher than their property values. They had no way of paying the mortgages and the banks were taking them to the cleaners.

They lost everything, and it was heartbreaking to see. They were bankrupt and were going through the painful process of starting all over again from a deep hole.

To their credit, they did just that. Many people would have given up and played victim. These two took responsibility, learned the lessons and got back to work.

The point is, you must always weigh the potential risks against the potential rewards for every opportunity and decision you make. Always weigh up the potential upside of an investment decision against the potential downside if things go wrong, and ask yourself if you could live with that?

I'm not suggesting you have to run a risk/reward analysis for every decision you make. Life could become both flavourless and stressful without the joy of spontaneity and the learnings you get from stuffing things up and getting to retry them in a different way. But by assessing decisions from a few different perspectives, your decision making, and ultimately your results, can shift beautifully.

You might find this framework works for all types of decisions, and not just your money-related ones. So what are some decisions you might be procrastinating on that you could get clear on using this framework?

Power points

- There are three types of knowledge in the world: stuff you know you know (KYK); stuff you know you don't know (KDK); and stuff you don't know you don't know (DKDK).

- When learning the language of money, there are three areas of focus: learn how to earn; learn how to grow what you earn; and learn how to keep what you grow.

- Relying on a single income stream is risky; two offer some security, three bring stability, and with more you enter the realm of abundance.

- If you don't get your money working hard for you, then you will spend your entire life working hard for money and stay trapped in the middle.

- Raising your financial IQ, at its core, means becoming a better financial decision maker.

- The quality of your life is based on the quality of your decisions, so you must look to increasing the quality of your financial decision making.

- The decision-making matrix engages three filters:

  - Filter #1: **Alignment.** Align financial decisions with your core values and top goals. Trusting your instincts and focusing on what matters most helps you avoid negative outcomes.

- Filter #2: **Highest outcomes**. Make decisions that align with your highest goals, regularly asking if a choice brings you closer, allowing you to embrace the right opportunities and avoid distractions.

- Filter #3: **Risk/reward ratio**. Every investment involves risk, so assess whether the potential reward justifies the possible downsides, keeping in mind that external factors may affect results beyond your control.

Meet Rodney

When I was young, I was taught that the only way to succeed in life was to just work hard. At 34, I had been doing just that for the past 16 years, first as a chef and then as a postie. Yet, despite putting aside some savings and a few shares, my wife and I had next to no assets and felt stuck in our jobs.

I always believed there had to be another way, but I had no idea how to find it.

Everything changed after I attended an event with Todd Polke. It became clear that there was a different pathway, and Todd held the key. Working with Todd has been an amazing experience. He makes growing wealth simple to understand and incredibly effective.

Just eight months into the journey, our financial situation and future looked completely different. I had minimised our expenses and was saving over 40 per cent of my income. Our first home was under construction, we had made our first property investment and we had started generating a monthly passive income of $1300 from various opportunities.

Fast forward to today, just four years later, and the transformation has been extraordinary. Our net worth has grown significantly, from virtually nothing to $1.6 million. We now have systems in place that work, insurances and financial buffers to protect us, and the peace of mind that our family would be cared for if anything were to happen to us.

I've learned how to identify high-income opportunities that generate strong returns without necessarily taking on high risks. This realisation was a game-changer for me—understanding that good returns don't always equate to high risk when approached strategically.

We now have six income streams. My main job is set to increase by $20 000 this year, my side hustle generates $500–$600 per week and the remaining streams come from our diversified investments. Our two properties have appreciated significantly, with one increasing from $606 000 to $945 000 and the other from $750 000 to $1.02 million, adding over $600 000 in equity. We've also invested in three high-growth business opportunities and a joint venture projected to return 55 per cent within two years.

But the real foundation of this transformation has been the system we learned from Todd. Setting clear financial goals, defining our financial freedom figure and learning to manage personal finances effectively laid the groundwork for everything else.

Through this journey, I've learned that so much more is possible than I ever imagined:

- That working hard isn't the only way to earn money.

- That investing isn't just for the rich—it's for anyone with the right knowledge and strategy.

- That building passive income is achievable.

- That saving becomes easy when you truly understand where your money is going.

And so much more.

This journey hasn't just changed our finances—it's transformed our lives. I feel less stressed and more in control. For the first time, my wife and I can enjoy life without constantly worrying about money. We're even going on a Disney cruise this December, something I never thought we could afford.

Thanks to Todd's guidance, I now have clarity about what I'm working toward, instead of wandering around aimlessly. Financial freedom is no longer a pipe dream—it's something I know I'll achieve in the next 5–8 years. I am almost out of the rat race!

PART IV

INSTALL YOUR PERSONAL FINANCE SYSTEM

CHAPTER 10

YOUR FINANCE FARM

Building wealth isn't about luck; it's about cultivating a system that works for you over time. Think of your finances as a thriving farm. Like any successful farm, it needs intentional planning, designated spaces for growth and consistent care to yield results. This chapter introduces the structure of your *finance farm*—a framework that organises your income, allocates it purposefully and prepares it for future growth.

I grew up on farms, and on a working farm everything (and everyone) has a job to do. There isn't room for inefficiencies or laziness. The land is prepared, crops are produced, harvests are gathered, with contingencies for rain and drought, and the land is taken care of to ensure future crops are fertile and sustainable.

Much the same applies to your personal financial system. It is a process where every dollar has a job to do, not only to help 'sustain life' but to prepare you for the future and protect you and your family, and generations to come if that is your plan.

In truth, everyone already has a financial system of some kind, but for many people the system is broken, which is one important reason why they are stuck in the middle. Money may be flowing in, but then it somehow magically evaporates into thin air. Imagine if every dollar is designated to a particular place to be nurtured and multiplied—and you can clearly see where each resource is going and why.

One key question on wealth building I introduce when teaching is this: 'Why would you be given more money to manage if you can't manage what you already have?' Just as crops flourish on well-maintained and -managed land, money tends to grow in places where order, structure and care are manifested. Money is drawn to fertile environments, where there is clear direction, intention and value.

This chapter will guide you through setting up your own finance farm in three essential phases:

1. **Production.** This initial phase is about *generating income*. Just as a farm works to produce a harvest, you're focused here on earning income, being clear about how much you have available in readiness to be divided into the different finance fields.
2. **Dividing the yield.** In this phase, you *allocate your income* to serve specific purposes across the three finance fields. Just as a farmer divides the harvest for various uses, you will be assigning portions of your income into three separate finance fields—sustainability, storage and seeding—ensuring each dollar has a plan and a purpose.
3. **Seeding for future growth.** In the final phase, funds set aside for *seeding* are used to invest for future growth. Like a farmer planting seeds for the next season, or investing in technology or more land to increase efficiency and yields, you invest these funds in assets, skill building or other growth opportunities to increase your future yield.

By the end of this chapter, you'll have designed a finance farm where every dollar is managed with purpose, is prepared for growth and contributes to your financial freedom.

Designing your financial flow

Before we get to cultivating your farm, you need to understand the current flow of money in your life. Your financial flow is basically what happens to your money after it hits your bank account. For most people, this is a fairly random process. Money comes in, usually from a job or business, and is then directed to what seems most pressing or urgent at the time, rather than to where it best serves you.

Figure 10.1 illustrates the typical money flow of someone stuck in the middle.

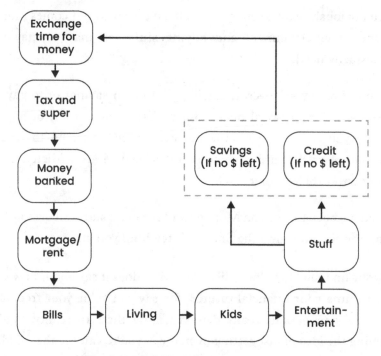

Figure 10.1: the default financial flow

Typically, you'll head off to work and give up your time in exchange for money. But before you even receive the money it will often have been plundered a few times. The tax department usually has first dibs. Depending on where you live, compulsory retirement savings such as superannuation in Australia, Kiwi Saver in New Zealand, 401k in the US, the Central Provident Fund (CPF) in Singapore, Pension schemes in the UK, the PRPP in Canada etc, are next.

Once what's left hits your bank account, paying for life takes over.

For most people, it first goes towards keeping a roof over their heads through a mortgage or rent. The utility bills, such as electricity and water, will come next. Once all that's settled, you'll need to pay for food, transportation, kids, car, insurance, rates, phone and more.

You obviously want to enjoy yourself a bit, so next out comes money spent on entertainment and buying stuff you may or may not necessarily need.

If you have any left over, that will go into your savings or to paying down existing personal debts. But perhaps you ran out of money before you ran out of month and are forced to get on the crack cocaine of credit cards, which so many people are addicted to in order cover the rest of it.

Then it's back to work on Monday and the cycle starts all over again. And round and round the financial treadmill you go.

If your financial flow looks like this, what does it say about how you are valuing your financial future? You say you value your freedom, but are your actions really demonstrating that? In reality, you're valuing the idea of just getting by in life—you're valuing the middle. This mindset isn't going to help you build wealth.

Let's say you're someone who has made the commitment to escape the middle and once and for all to value financial freedom in your life—not because of the money, of course, but because of the choices that financial freedom can give you. What would be one thing you could do that would begin shifting this flow?

Answer: you would *pay yourself first*. You're probably familiar with this expression, but are you actually doing it? If you are, congratulations—it's a powerful financial habit. If not, what has been holding you back?

Ten per cent of your income is the common amount suggested. As soon as your income hits your bank account, 10 per cent is automatically transferred to your savings so you are paying yourself first then living on the other 90 per cent.

You might say, 'Todd, you don't get it. I can't pay 10 per cent; I'm not making enough money!' So start with 5 per cent, 3 per cent or even just 1 per cent! The amount matters less than building the habit of investing in yourself and your future.

Put a plan in place. If you start with 1 per cent in the first month, set up an automatic transfer as soon as your income hits your account. Make it easy and automatic. In month two, increase it to 2 per cent, then 3 per cent in month three, and so on. By the end of the year, you'll be setting aside 10 per cent, or even more of your income. Not only will you have built a cash buffer and the start of an investment portfolio, but you'll have achieved a savings goal you might initially have thought impossible. This practice is the beginning of training your mind towards wealth and freedom.

You're creating the habit of paying yourself and the mindset of growing wealth. This is where wealth is built—not just on the big one-off actions you take, but on the small and strategic habits repeated consistently over time.

A couple I worked with applied this principle. Carlos and Maria first came to me and complained, using the words I have heard so often before, 'Todd, we just can't seem to save any money. We keep trying to put away 10 per cent, but then we run out before the end of the month or something comes up, and we keep dipping into it. It just doesn't work for us.'

I reminded them that wealth is a marathon, not a sprint, and that their future success will be built on the firm foundations they construct right now. Rather than focusing on big things to begin with, I suggested they get back to the foundational elements.

We put in place a 1 per cent plan, and to their credit they committed to it and followed through; in month two they upped it to 2 per cent and achieved that. It might not sound like much, but we were making progress. In months three, four and five they increased by a further 1 per cent each time, and now they had momentum.

Something interesting happened in month six. Carlos and Maria had had five months of achieving what they had thought they never could. They had set a savings plan and stuck to it. Their confidence was higher, they knew they could actually accomplish it, and they could see that saving towards their future was quite doable. So in month six they upped their monthly savings goal to 10 per cent of their income—and they achieved it, despite their previous failure.

As a part of the overall plan, we installed strategies to help Carlos and Maria at the same time gradually increase their incomes. Again, they committed and committed hard, and as their incomes grew so did their savings rate.

Fast forward to 12 months after this conversation and they were putting away 40 per cent of their new income. And it all began with that very modest 1 per cent target in month one.

Suffice to say, Carlos and Maria's financial lives and futures were looking very different at this point.

Remember, small, strategic actions taken consistently can grow to unexpected outcomes. There's a reason they say compound interest is the eighth wonder of the world. Its power can be unstoppable.

When you combine this new financial flow with your efforts to increase your income, you'll find you can reach your wealth goals much faster. Everyone can do this. No excuses.

Sadly, though, most people are more committed to their excuses in life than to their results and are left wondering why they are not getting the outcomes they desire. Commit to the practices that serve you, not to those that keep you stuck.

Mapping your current money flow

It can be hard to know where you're going if you don't know where you are right now. This isn't just about your finances, but also about your habits and processes. Understanding how your money moves reveals patterns in your spending and allocation. By identifying these habits, you can decide whether to keep them or change them.

Let's map out your current flow, before going to work on redesigning your money map towards wealth building.

Grab a pen and paper and draw a simple flow diagram (similar to the one in figure 10.1, page 159) to trace the general journey of your money before it hits your bank account. What gets paid first... and then what... and keep going until there's nothing left to track, taking note of what you are prioritising and why.

So how did you do? What did you notice? How would you like to do things differently?

Back to the farm

Let's now talk about how to get your finance farm operational. You can find a downloadable template at www.escapethemiddle.com.

As you complete your finance farm and refine it in the future you are going to want to get clear on some of your personal numbers so you can be as accurate as possible, but to begin with just give it your best guess (see figure 10.2). Remember habit #15: *Millionaire investors are master implementers*. Time to put this into practice.

So let's talk now about how to complete your finance farm.

Phase 1. Production

In this phase, your farm is in *production mode*. Based on your skills, training and experience you already know how to prepare the land and plant certain types of seeds in the soil. These seeds yield crops—your primary income from work or business efforts.

As you harvest each crop, some of your yield goes to common expenses, such as taxes and compulsory retirement contributions, before it reaches your account.

To begin, follow these steps:

- **Step 1.** Start by recording your *gross income* in the income box (1). This is your total earnings before deductions.
- **Step 2.** Next, note how much of your income goes to taxes and enter this in the tax box (2).
- **Step 3.** Then identify any compulsory retirement savings (such as superannuation) and record this in retirement savings box (3).

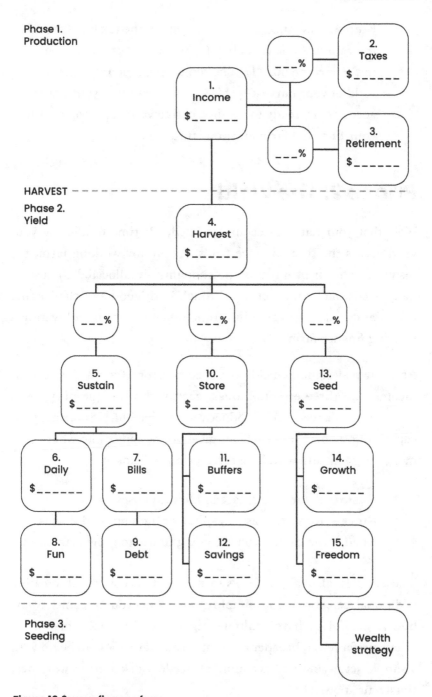

Figure 10.2: your finance farm

- **Step 4.** Now subtract the amounts in the tax box (2) and the retirement savings box (3) from your gross income in the income box (1). The remaining amount is the true yield of your harvest—this is what flows into your harvest account (4), ready to be allocated towards other aspects of your financial farm and your future.

Phase 2. The yield

Now that your harvest account is filled, it's time to allocate your yield across the three finance fields. As on any working farm, the resources you bring in must be thoughtfully allocated to sustain daily needs, maintain security through both good and challenging times, and fuel future growth—fundamental steps in cultivating a thriving finance farm.

As a farm designates fields for specific crops, you'll divide your income into three essential areas, each with a unique purpose to support a balanced and productive financial life. Splitting your capital across these finance fields gives you visibility into where your money is going and why. The three primary fields are:

- **Sustain**—for taking care of life's expenses
- **Store**—for setting aside capital for life's ups and downs
- **Seed**—the capital you are going to use to grow your future.

These fields also allow for 'sub-fields' or accounts, if creating additional categories will simplify managing your income. Some find it helpful to have multiple, tightly focused accounts, while others prefer fewer, broader accounts. You may choose to begin with a simple setup and add accounts as needed, discovering what best suits your approach.

Each account may also need varying levels of access: some might require a debit card for daily expenses, while others could be designated for online transfers only. I've provided suggestions based on what has worked for me and others. The point is to tailor this so you can craft a system that works for you.

Let's get started on setting up each field and assigning your income, ensuring every dollar has a purpose and a place in cultivating your financial future.

Field 1: Sustain

The *Sustain* field represents the essential investments that keep a farm—and your financial life—running smoothly. Just as a farm allocates resources to sustain its daily operations, care for its workers and maintain the health of livestock, your *Sustain* field covers the foundational costs of living. This field includes essentials such as housing, bills and groceries as well as healthcare and daily entertainment.

The *Sustain* field is all about supporting your everyday needs, ensuring you can live comfortably and maintain stability. By prioritising these core expenses, you lay the groundwork for a balanced financial farm that can support your life and wellbeing.

- **Step 5.** Set your Sustain percentage and amount. Get clear on how much you need to cover your living expenses, including to house and feed yourself and your family, and to pay utilities and other expenses. Your total amount will go in the Sustain box (5).

Above this you will see a box with a percentage sign, where you will allocate a certain percentage of your income to this finance field, so you can keep track of the trends of how much you are spending on living expenses, especially if your *Store* and *Seed* fields are left wanting.

For most people this will range between 50 and 70 per cent of their incomes.

- **Step 6. Choose your subaccounts.** There are four subaccount options you may or may not choose to add. These are designed to help you manage your specific expenses more intentionally. The Daily and Bills subaccounts will be your primary Sustain accounts, but some choose to use all of them for greater visibility and control.

Following are subaccount options.

Subaccount #1: Daily spending (6)

Purpose: This is an everyday account for essentials such as food and transportation, providing easy access to funds when you're out and about.

Access: You will want an account with a debit card so you have the flexibility and access to funds for day-to-day spending.

Subaccount #2: Bills (7)

Purpose: Set up an account for paying bills, keeping it separate from your daily spending. This ensures you always have enough to cover expenses and avoid surprises. Use this account for direct debits or scheduled transfers during your money management routine.

Access: This can be an online account only. Generally, no debit card access is required.

Subaccount #3: Entertainment (8)

Purpose: This account is for spending on entertainment and discretionary purchases. Transfer a set amount here, and enjoy spending it guilt free, knowing you're not dipping into other funds. Once it's gone, it's gone, but it's comforting to have money set aside for life's little indulgences.

Access: You'll want an account with a debit card so you have the flexibility and access for your spending blowout days.

Subaccount #4: Debt (9)

Purpose: This account is useful for tackling personal debt as part of your wealth plan. Allocate funds here to pay off high-interest debt first, helping you eliminate bad debt efficiently.

Access: This can be an online account only, and generally no debit card access is required.

- **Step 7. Fill in your numbers.** How much each pay cycle are you allocating towards each of your subaccounts to keep them topped up and ready to handle any expenses that may come your way? Start with your best guess, then refine these numbers as you gain more clarity about your situation.

Field 2: Store

The *Store* field is where farmers set aside part of their harvest for future needs, providing a safety net against droughts, feed shortages or unexpected challenges. For your financial farm, Store represents the buffers and savings that give you peace of mind. Just as a well-stocked storage field protects a farm, setting aside emergency funds ensures you're prepared for any unplanned expenses, whether related to work, health or family.

This field also includes savings for major purchases, such as vacations or a new car. By setting aside funds here, you're creating a reserve to draw on as life's larger needs arise, adding stability and flexibility to your financial life and reducing the impact of any surprises down the road that you haven't planned for.

- **Step 8. Set your Store percentage and amount.** How much capital are you setting aside as your buffers and to ensure you have the cash you need to cover future big-ticket payments you are saving towards?

You will need two accounts here, with the option of a third one if it makes sense to you. Typically, this will range between 50 and 70 per cent of your income.

Subaccount options include the following.

Subaccount #1: Buffers

Purpose: This account, also known as the s**t happens buffer, serves as your personal buffer for unexpected events. Life is unpredictable, and having a financial cushion helps you navigate tough times with less stress. I usually like to have six months of living expenses tucked aside, but you can adapt this to your needs. Choose a figure that gives you a sense of security—perhaps a certain number of months of living expenses set aside that in the event of a crisis would buy you time to sort your life out again. Set your figure and begin allocating towards it.

Access: Regular access to withdraw from this account is not needed and nor is it recommended. A no-fee online account is preferable.

- **Step 8. Calculate your buffer.** Let's do the sums. First, what are your monthly living expenses? Next, how many months of living expenses do you want to set aside so you know that in a crisis you'll be safe financially?

Multiply these two together. For example, if your monthly living expenses figure is $4000 and you want six months of living expenses stacked aside, then it would look simply like:

$4000 \times 6 \, months = \$24\,000$

Add this into the Buffer box (11).

Access: Regular access to withdraw from this account is not recommended. A no-fee online account is preferable.

Subaccount #2: Savings

Purpose: Savings are funds set aside for known expenses or larger purchases, such as a holiday, a new car or a skills course.

- **Step 9. Setting aside your savings.** Look ahead one or two years, list upcoming major expenses for bigger ticket items, estimate their costs, count how many months you have until the target and determine how much you need to save regularly to reach your goal.

It will look something like table 10.1.

Table 10.1: savings calculation for big-ticket items

Goal	Total cost	# of months	Monthly savings
Holiday	$6500.00	10	$650.00
New car	$25 000.00	18	$1388.88
		Monthly total	<u>$2038.88</u>

By laying it out like this you can clearly see whether or not this savings goal is achievable, given the distributions into the other finance fields you need to make, and whether you need to adjust some of your targets.

This will now go into your Savings box (12).

Access: Regular access to withdraw from this account is not recommended. A no-fee online account is preferable.

Field 3: Seed

The *Seed* field is where a farm sets aside its seeds for future planting. Farmers allocate resources here to acquire more land, expand livestock, invest in new seeds or improve efficiency through new technology and expertise, all aimed at increasing production and yields. In your financial life, the *Seed* field represents funds set aside for future growth and wealth building.

This field covers investments in assets, as well as self-investment to boost skills and financial knowledge, enhancing the potential to earn more. By nurturing your *Seed* field, you're planting the seeds for a prosperous financial future, positioning yourself for long-term growth and abundance.

The subaccounts include the following:

Subaccount #1: Growth fund

Purpose: The Growth fund is where you set aside money to invest back into your own growth and evolution. This could be for learning new skills or gaining qualifications to increase your earning potential, for raising your financial and investing IQ, or for becoming more effective and efficient in the business called *you*.

Access: Online access is usually enough.

- **Step 10. Fund your growth.** You will have heard me say already that if you want to grow your wealth, focus on growing yourself first and be strategic about it.

Where in your life do you want or need to develop and evolve? Is it in education, learning a new skill, gaining a new certification or investing in a network?

If you were to level yourself up in that area, would it have a significant impact on your earning potential and wealth creation, or in you as a person? It could look something like table 10.2. Again, you now have a monthly amount to add in your Growth box (14) as you grow and expand who you are.

Table 10.2: calculating growth expenses

Growth goal	Total cost	# of months	Monthly savings amount to reach
Financial education	$4000.00	6	$666.67
Learn sales	$6000.00	20	$300.00
		Monthly total	$966.67

Subaccount #2: Freedom fund

Purpose: The Freedom fund is where you set aside money to invest and grow your portfolio, creating long-term financial freedom. This is your 'pay yourself first' fund, for building towards major investments, such as a property deposit or dollar-cost averaging into shares, funds or crypto. Consistent contributions here are key to your future financial independence. As you build up capital in this field you will deploy it according to your own personal wealth-building strategy to accelerate your journey towards your financial freedom.

Access: Online access is usually enough.

- **Step 11. Fill your freedom fund.** What is the amount you have committed to set aside to invest in your future wealth? This is the epitome of paying yourself first and the more you invest here, the better.

This is the fund you are going to build up and then begin deploying into assets and income streams for your future (you'll have the opportunity to plan and action this in later chapters).

Choose your amount. Are you able to invest 10 per cent of your income towards your future, or do you need to begin with the 1 per cent plan, like Carlos and Maria? Or are you pushing towards 20 per cent or 40 per cent or more?

Whatever figure you choose, add it in Freedom box (15).

Phase 3. Sowing

In this final phase, your focus shifts to *sowing the seeds* for future growth. Just as a farmer plants seeds in prepared soil to yield the best crops for future seasons, you'll invest the resources in your *Seed* field to create lasting financial growth. This phase is all about using your capital to acquire assets, develop income streams and expand your financial portfolio, setting the foundation for financial freedom.

By carefully selecting where to plant these 'seeds'—whether in investments, property, skill building or other growth opportunities. You're cultivating resources that will yield returns in the future. Like a well-planned crop cycle, this sowing process ensures that your financial farm not only sustains you today but continues to grow and thrive, season after season.

The chapters that follow will show you how to sow your seeds for your future.

A few points on making this work

An effective personal finance system requires you to know yourself and, when necessary, protect yourself from yourself. If you tend to spend impulsively, limit your access to capital to avoid dipping into funds meant for other commitments. Be honest as you redesign your money map and create a financial flow that aligns with your goals.

None of us is perfect; we all have habits and vices that can undermine our progress. Recognising these tendencies allows you to set up systems that prevent 'bad' habits from undoing your good work.

This is why it's also important to get clear about how much it actually costs you to live daily, so you can set a realistic budget. This way, you won't need to withdraw unnecessary amounts from your other accounts.

If you're still living paycheque to paycheque, your first goal is to set aside $1000 in a dedicated account and leave it untouched. This small buffer provides security for emergencies or unexpected expenses. While it may seem a trifling amount, having even this cushion creates a sense of safety and confidence. It shows both you, yourself and the universe that you can manage money and so attract more abundance into your life.

Restructuring your money map helps you build better financial habits, knowing that every dollar is working harder for you. Now every dollar has a plan and a purpose.

You've mapped your flow and can add this to your 'money night' process. Now it's time to plug the financial leaks to retain even more of your cashflow.

Power points

- There are no secrets to success, only systems.

- Wealth isn't about luck; it's about creating a system. Like a thriving farm, your finances need purposeful planning, designated spaces for growth, and consistent care to produce results.

- Your finance farm is a framework that organises your income, allocates it purposefully and prepares it for future growth.

- The finance farm philosophy: Every dollar needs a plan and a purpose, without which it will evaporate.

- Why would you be given more money to manage if you can't manage what you already have?

- The three phases of your finance farm are:

  1. **Production,** focusing on generating income, forming the foundation for purposeful distribution

  2. **Dividing the yield,** when income is allocated across three targeted finance fields:

     - The *Sustain* field covers essential expenses like housing, food and bills, with optional subaccounts for daily spending, bills, entertainment and debt.

     - The *Store* field builds a financial buffer for emergencies or large planned purchases.

     - The *Seed* field funds future growth through self-improvement and investments.

  3. **Sowing for future growth,** investing funds from the Seed field, channelling capital into assets and opportunities to achieve long-term financial freedom.

- Are you claiming to value freedom, yet letting your actions tell a different story?

- We don't value wealth building because of the money itself, but because of the choices it opens up.

- Wealth is built not through big, one-time actions, but through small, strategic habits repeated consistently over time.

- An effective personal finance system requires self-awareness and, when needed, safeguards against your own tendencies. If you're prone to impulsive spending, limit access to certain funds to protect your financial commitments.

- Cultivating your finance farm turns every dollar into a future asset, making each financial choice a step towards financial independence.

CHAPTER 11

FINANCIAL INEFFICIENCIES ARE KILLING YOU

Have you ever experienced the mystery of evaporating money, when money comes into your life then seems to just magically disappear, and you have no idea where it has gone?

A lot of people go through this *every month*. In chapter nine we talked about your 'river of wealth'; where your primary income stream flows from its source towards the main riverbed where your wealth can be created. Before it gets there, though, the harsh sun and unstable river walls soak it all up, leaving you with barely a trickle, or nothing at all, to begin investing with. Like the inefficiencies on your finance farm, this too leads to wasted money, wasted time and wasted opportunity.

Plug the leaks

To stop this loss from happening you need to fine-tune your financial life. This means plugging the leaks that are causing you to lose money so you can better manage every dollar that goes into your finance fields.

Management expert Peter Drucker suggests, 'You can't manage what you don't measure.' Drucker's idea is straightforward. Running a business involves taking care of your numbers, including your cashflow, sales and expenses.

Think of your personal finance in a similar way. You are basically running your own personal finance business. The important thing here is that you need to apply the same mindset. This can seem really boring to many people, especially those who want to skip the basics and go straight to the more interesting parts like buying assets and growing income streams.

But if you don't have a system in place for managing money when it comes in, it *will* leak out. Think back to your first full-time salary. When you kept working that job and received your first raise, what did you notice? If you're like most people, it probably would have been that somehow your living expenses went up by exactly the same amount.

Magic!

Or was it that you didn't have a system, so your money just leaked out? Remember, if you can't manage what you already have, why would you be given more money to manage?

Conducting a financial audit can be a very powerful (and profitable) process.

Ask this simple question: *In which area of my financial life can I be more effective and efficient?* Then leave no stone unturned in addressing the question wherever you interact with money. You may be shocked by how much you find you are simply giving away because you are not being efficient.

I conduct a financial audit every six months. This involves creating a list of all my regular expenses then doing the research to look for better deals. Invariably I'll find at least one area where I can squeeze out some more dollars.

Rodney is a mini celebrity among our investor groups, not only because he has grown a million-dollar portfolio in just a couple of short years, but because he's a monster at plugging his financial leaks.

We ran a 'Plug the Leaks' challenge in our community. Everyone had one week to save as much money as they could using the system we provided. The average participant saved an extra $500 per month. The winner of the challenge saved a whopping $2250 per month, or $27000 per year. The highest so far took that number up to $45000! Surely that's better in your back pocket than in the hands of big corporations.

Having given them all the tools and scripts and spreadsheets they needed to make it happen, here are the steps we took them through:

1. Compile a list of every regular expenditure over a six-month period, such as bills, fees, repayments and mortgages. Six months means you capture outgoings, such as quarterly electricity bills. (You can download a spreadsheet version at www.escapethemiddle.com.)
2. Get clear on the current amounts you are spending on these so you have a target to beat.
3. Do your research on the competitors who could be vying for your business and check out their best current deals. Comparison websites can be exceptionally useful for

accounts, loans, insurances and much more. This research equips you with data with which you can negotiate.

4. Call your current provider. Here's a sample script I use:

Hi. My name is Todd Polke. I've been a customer of yours for the past three years. I've just been doing some research to find some better deals as things are getting pretty expensive. What can you do for me to help me lower my bill?

[They will likely run through their other options and plans.]

So xyz company is offering this right now [tell them the deal], which would save me $____ each year. Are you able to beat that?

I want to stay with you. I've been a loyal customer, but things are tight at the moment and I need to find some ways to save some money.

[Let them talk. They may or may not come up with a better offer.]

You have some choices now:

a. It's a good offer and you want to proceed: 'Great, thank you. Can we set that up now please?'

b. It's a good deal, but you still want to do some more research: 'Great, thank you. Could you please email that over to me so I can… ['check with my partner' or 'make sure I can afford it before I commit' — and so on.]'

c. It's not a good deal: 'Unless there's anything else you can do, can you switch me over to your cancellations team, please?'

Note that these people have a lot of power, and they know it's cheaper to keep a customer than sign up a new one so they can often offer other options. Tell them about what their competitors are offering and the savings you'll make and let them go to work. And if they really can't do anything, go chat with their competitors and find a better deal elsewhere.

5. Plan where you will reallocate the savings. A dollar without a plan is wasted, whether by the creep effect of inflation or by being spent on things of low value. Have a plan for every dollar you save so it's put to work. Perhaps it's to pay down high-interest debt, or to put towards your 'sleep soundly' factor or into your freedom fund.

Plugging your financial leaks requires some upfront time investment and some messing around, but the compound effect of the savings can be exceptional. You've gotta love the power of compounding!

Simultaneously, you can implement strategies to grow your income then compound your increased income with your savings and more efficient finance system, and watch your results surge forward.

To be clear, this doesn't mean not enjoying and experiencing life; rather, it is a call to be smarter with your money and to manage it better for your future benefit. Trying to build wealth while living on baked beans and rice sucks. I do not recommend it. Enjoy life and create more resources to increase your level of experience of it all. The point is to be smart, intentional and efficient. Without financial discipline, you won't achieve financial freedom. Do the work to set up the system, then watch the system deliver compound results for you over time.

Automate your flow

Once you're clear on your money map and financial flow, the next step is to optimise the process to make it easier for you. Wealth building isn't about constantly monitoring your budget; it's about creating a system that does the work for you.

The key is automation. Leverage technology to handle your income, bills and investments. There are now plenty of secure tools that can help to manage your finances for you. By automating your financial flow, you step into the top 1 per cent of personal money managers. This allows you to focus on living your life and expanding your wealth.

Systemise, automate and schedule as much as possible for maximum efficiency.

If you want to save 10 per cent of your income, set up an automatic transfer that grabs it as soon as it arrives. With your expenses on autopilot, you won't need to think about them throughout the week. Credit card, rent, mortgage or loans—you can automate almost any type of account. Check with your bank or service provider on how to streamline the process.

By becoming more financially disciplined and organised, and letting technology handle the routine tasks, you free up time and mental energy, allowing you to focus on growing your wealth. This is one of the six key levers of leverage we'll discuss later in the book.

By automating your financial flow, you step into the top 1 per cent, because very few people manage their personal finances this way. Once you do this consistently, you'll find more cash stays in your pocket rather than flowing elsewhere. This can be used to improve your lifestyle, grow your wealth or even pay down debt, which is the subject of the next chapter.

Power points

- Having organised your finance farm, now it's time to plug the financial leaks in your life and optimise the output of your finance system.

- Do this by conducting a financial audit. One powerful question to ask is: *In this area of my financial life, can I be more effective and efficient?*

- Treat your finances like a business. Manage it seriously, and you'll see serious results. Treat it like a hobby, and expect hobby-level results.

- Steps to conducting a financial audit:

  1. Compile a list of every regular expenditure over a six-month period.

  2. Get clear on the current amounts you are spending on these, so you have a target to beat.

  3. Do your research on the competitors who could be vying for your business, and check out their best current deals.

  4. Call your current provider to negotiate.

  5. Plan where you will reallocate the savings.

- Without financial discipline, you won't achieve financial freedom.

- Do the work to set up the system upfront, then watch it deliver compound results for you over time.

- By becoming more financially disciplined and organised, and letting technology handle the routine tasks, you free up time and mental energy, allowing you to focus on growing your wealth. This is one of the six key levers of leverage.

CHAPTER 12

DEALING WITH DEBT

Debt can be your best financial ally or your worst enemy, depending on how you use it. For some, it leads to financial ruin, while for others, it accelerates the path to financial freedom. Like money, debt isn't inherently good or bad; it's just a thing. Its impact depends on the hands that wield it. If you act with your credit like a drunken monkey with a knife, then you endanger yourself and your financial future. However, used responsibly and intelligently, debt becomes leverage—one of the key tools for building wealth and success, allowing you to tap into resources well beyond your own.

It's time to reconsider your relationship with debt. Debt isn't inherently bad; it depends on your purpose and intention. Reflect on these questions:

- What is your current relationship with debt?
- Has your experience with debt been empowering or painful?
- Where did your understanding of debt come from?
- What does your use of debt reveal about your money management?

Good debt versus bad debt

There is good debt and bad debt. Whether a debt is good or bad has much to do with the role it plays in your life. Does the debt you take on have the potential to empower you financially in the future? Or does it disempower you?

Bad debt typically includes debt accumulated for consumption purposes, including:

- personal loans
- car loans
- credit card debts
- store cards
- store financing.

Good debt is used to acquire assets, such as:

- lending for investment properties
- financial investment in courses and training programs to increase your income or net worth
- investment loans for shares, funds etc.
- business loans.

I'm often asked whether your own home represents good or bad debt. To answer, ask yourself: does your home have the potential to financially empower or disempower you?

Some people overspend on a house, ending up with crippling debt that disrupts their financial lives. Others make responsible decisions, turning their homes into a cornerstone of future wealth. This can happen through capital gains, accessing equity for future investments or simply providing a stable financial foundation, which can be incredibly empowering.

In essence, bad debt is often used for consumption purposes, whereas good debt is often used for investment. Here's the tricky part, though; a good debt can turn into a bad debt if you make a poor decision. Originally you took a loan with the intention of creating financial empowerment; if the decision begins to financially disempower you, then it becomes a bad debt.

Should you carry ongoing debt? If it's personal (bad) debt, then no, get the hell rid of it. If it's investment (good) debt, use it for a period responsibly and always have a plan to manage it and pay it back as part of your strategy. Ultimately you will likely want to own your assets outright even if this is in a later phase of your portfolio building.

Debt is not a financial problem; it's a people problem.

Yes, life throws challenges our way. I've been there too. For most people, however, debt isn't caused by those unexpected events. It stems from habits of poor financial management and an addiction to consumerism and instant gratification. Many buy things they don't need to impress others or feel good in the moment, only to be left with sleepless nights, financial stress and a lingering debt hangover that can't be fixed with a quick remedy.

To tackle debt once and for all, you must address its root causes; otherwise, you're only treating the symptoms.

A shift in focus

You get what you focus on. It seems to be a law of the universe. Don't believe me? Think of the last time you hurt your foot or hand. You probably focused on it while taking care not to bump it. But despite your best efforts to protect it, you seemed to hit everything in sight, drop things on it, knock or run into everything you possibly could! Maybe it's just me, but it's a rule I just can't escape!

Dealing with debt requires shifting your focus away from the debt itself and its causes, and instead adopting a solution-oriented mindset.

Focusing on the debt and its impact only makes you feel worse. In that negative state, it becomes difficult to see through the fog and find solutions beyond slowly paying it back, bit by bit.

When you focus only on debt solutions, you're treating the symptom, not the cause. Your focus should rather be on changing your habits, beliefs and behaviours around money. By changing your financial lifestyle, the external symptoms (debt and financial stress) will start to dissipate sustainably.

This doesn't mean you ignore debt management solutions—you absolutely need them. But to truly change your financial future, the focus must start with you. Addressing your attitudes and habits tackles the root cause, allowing the symptoms to resolve without intense self-discipline or deprivation.

Dealing with bad debt in your life

Are you stuck in bad debt and ready to break free? It all starts with a plan—a random approach rarely works.

Here's a step-by-step guide you can start to apply right now.

1. Get off the credit drug

If overspending got you into debt, it's time for a personal debt detox by cutting out credit spending. Remove temptation; otherwise, old habits will return and sabotage your progress. Cut up your credit cards, or if you must keep one, place it in a container of water and freeze it. That way, any use will require the hassle of breaking it out of the ice, giving you time to reconsider!

2. Get clear on what you owe

Open a spreadsheet and list every debt and:

- who it's with
- how much it is
- what the interest rate is
- minimum monthly payments
- how long it will take to pay off, based on your current repayments.

3. Choose which debt to tackle first

There are three strategies to consider.

Deal with the urgent

Some debts are more pressing than others—those with collectors involved, for example. Ignoring them won't help, so prioritise handling these first to avoid mounting costs and protect your credit record. Consider negotiating new terms with creditors to make these debts more manageable.

High-interest first

From a financial perspective, start with the debt carrying the highest interest rate. Pay the minimum on other debts while focusing on this one to save the most money in the long run.

Lowest balance first

For a psychological boost, tackle the smallest debt first. Clearing smaller balances gives a sense of progress and builds momentum, turning debt reduction into a challenge rather than a burden. Use this momentum to fuel your future wealth-building efforts.

4. Set your hit list and order your debts accordingly

Once you have decided which option will best suit you to begin with—whether the most pressing, the highest interest or the lowest balance—go back and order your spreadsheet accordingly. You now have your hit list.

5. Free up cash by plugging the leaks

You have already done the plug-the-leaks exercise and you have likely found some spare cashflow in your life. Decide how much you are going to be committing towards debt elimination.

6. Transfer balances to lower your interest rate profile

Anywhere you can, adjust your interest rate from a higher to a lower level. For credit cards, look at balance transfers to get extended interest-free periods, freeing up even more cash to begin compounding that debt down.

7. Readjust your money map and shift your flow

Update your money map and your cashflow. Direct your spare cashflow towards the right account and then automate it. Take human error out of the equation and let technology do the work for you.

8. Snowball it, ploughing the debts over

Pay the minimum on all debts except the one you're targeting first; add the extra cashflow directly into that. Once that's cleared, take what you were paying on it, plus any extra cash, and focus on the next debt. Repeat the process, combining payments from each cleared debt into the next. This creates a snowball effect, rapidly reducing your balances and bringing a satisfying sense of progress.

9. Shift your focus — you get what you focus on

With your debt plan in place, stop obsessing over it. Instead, focus on creating more abundance in your life to accelerate debt elimination. Here's how:

- **Increase efficiency.** Identify where you're wasting money and streamline your finances. Create a budget, negotiate lower rates on bills and audit your expenses to manage your money like a well-oiled machine.
- **Grow your income**. Upskill to increase your market value and earn more for your efforts.

10. Reallocate — shift from debt reduction to wealth creation

Now you've eliminated your debt, you have extra cashflow. What will you do to change your financial future? Add it to your buffers or your freedom fund to put it to work for you.

Notice, this isn't about scarcity. I don't believe in building wealth while living on the bare minimum. It's about creating more and growing as a person and wealth creator. This mindset shift is key to becoming truly wealthy.

But what about the debt on your home? Paying off a mortgage through the bank's 25+-year plan is a poor strategy. You're playing by their rules, making them richer while you keep paying. This advice is often handed out by banks, brokers and even family members, but don't just accept it. Question it.

Many professionals, even those with certifications, lack real investing experience. I know, I've worked with many of them as clients and have helped them grow their portfolios. Qualifications mean little; what matters is their results, experience and who they've helped.

Personally, I use profits from my investment portfolio to pay off my home debt in large chunks through what I call the Momentum Strategy (explained in chapter 14). I leverage home equity to grow income streams and acquire more assets, then trade some back to the market. This excess cashflow is used to quickly pay down the home debt, offering a faster path to financial freedom.

Leverage for wealth building

This raises the other reason you might choose to take on debt—to grow your wealth by leveraging other people's money (OPM) rather than needing to come up with all the cash yourself.

When used correctly, debt can be a powerful tool for leverage, which is why I prefer to call it leverage rather than debt. This mindset shift is crucial when using it to grow your wealth. By putting down a small deposit and using OPM to fund the rest, you can access assets of greater value than you could otherwise.

Leverage can be applied to building investment portfolios through margin lending, stock trading or business acquisitions, but let's focus on its use in property. For instance, buying a property worth $500000 would require significant savings if you had to pay the full amount. Many would be locked out of the market, especially with today's cost-of-living issues. However, being able to put down a 10 per cent, 20 per cent or 30 per cent deposit ($50k to $150k) and finance the rest opens up opportunities that might otherwise be out of reach.

Of course, this means additional monthly expenses for loan repayment, so it's crucial to understand the consequences and have a strategy in place. Ultimately it comes down to a simple question: *Will this move bring me closer to my goals?* That is, *does the benefit outweigh the risks, and can I handle the downside if things go wrong?*

Become comfortable with debt

This flies in the face of the common dogma about debt. We are often told to avoid it at all costs; when used strategically, however, it can be a great tool. I am more than happy to be millions of dollars in debt leveraged into solid investments. I hold solid assets, my portfolio cashflow supports the debt with a hefty buffer in place and I have a plan to eliminate it.

All wealth creation requires a strategy—whether it's for investments, taxes, finance, loans, diversification or income. This includes a debt reduction strategy.

With a solid plan in place, debt loses its emotional weight and simply becomes a tool. You decide how, and if, you want to use it.

Power points

- Debt can be your best ally or your worst enemy; depending on how you use it, it can lead to financial ruin or fast-track your journey to financial freedom.

- Like money, debt isn't inherently good or bad; it's just a thing. Its impact depends on the hands that wield it.

- Good debt can empower your financial future.

- Bad debt can disempower your financial future.

- In essence, bad debt is often used for consumption purposes, whereas good debt is often used for investment.

- Debt is not a financial problem; it's a people problem.

- Focusing solely on debt solutions addresses the symptoms, not the root cause. Instead, shift your focus to changing your habits, beliefs and behaviours around money.

- How to deal with bad debt in your life:

  - Get off the credit drug.

  - Get clear on what you owe.

  - Choose which debt to tackle first.

  - Set your hit list and order your debts accordingly.

  - Free up cash by plugging the leaks.

  - Transfer balances to lower your interest rate profile.

  - Readjust your money map and shift your flow.

  - Snowball it, ploughing the debts over.

  - Shift your focus—you get what you focus on.

  - Reallocate, shifting from debt reduction to wealth creation.

- Paying off a mortgage through the bank's 25-year plan is a poor strategy. You're playing by their rules, making them richer while you keep paying.

- When choosing whether to take on debt, ask:

  - *Will this move bring me closer to my goals?*

  - *Does the benefit outweigh the risks, and can I handle the downside if things go wrong?*

- All wealth creation requires a strategy, whether it's for investments, taxes, finance, loans, diversification or income. This includes debt reduction.

- With a solid plan in place, debt loses its emotional weight and simply becomes a tool. You decide how, and if, you want to use it.

PART V

SAY NO TO LAZY MONEY

CHAPTER 13

GETTING STARTED WITH INVESTING

If you don't get your money working hard for you, you'll spend your entire life just working hard for money—and stuck in the middle. You must get yourself invested, so your money grows for you while you sleep.

But what do we mean when we say 'invested'? Most will associate it with putting money into some assets, whether property or shares, crypto or gold. And although that is absolutely a part of it, it's also a very limited view of what investing is, a view that will likely lead to sub-par results or, worse, expensive mistakes.

Early in the book I pointed out that your investing journey begins well before you buy your first asset. The assets you invest in are like the tip of the iceberg, the shiny thing you see above the surface, whereas the majesty of your portfolio, and the foundation of your success, is in all the elements beneath the surface.

This is a journey we have already begun in this book, first by turning on your millionaire mode—your mindset—then by learning to understand the money game of life and raising your financial IQ through education.

We'll continue to build on the following foundations as you prepare to make your first—or next—investment:

- **Team**—how to choose and structure your six-star wealth team
- **Strategy**—how to understand the seven portfolio-building pillars and the three strategies every investor needs in their portfolio
- **Finance**—how to use lending safely and effectively to grow your portfolio (and pay it back afterwards)
- **Structure**—how to build your financial fortress so you stay safe while building wealth.

Finally, as we breach the surface, it's time to ask how to find the deals that will make the difference in your portfolio by earning you more profits and cashflow.

All these elements are part of the Full Circle Strategy System I'll share with you further in the next chapter. It may sound like a lot to get your head around, and it is. There's a lot to consider when you're building a portfolio leading you towards financial freedom, but getting started does not need to be complex at all. In fact, I think you should just get on with it.

Start small and build up, but start. Something magical happens when you take that first step and get invested in the market. Stepping away from the middle and towards your future is a powerful move, and with it comes an empowered energy that can propel you into momentum.

Normalising wealth creation

By getting invested, even in only a modest way, you are training your mind that this is your new direction, this is the new you.

You have the courage to set off towards your goals. Knowing that you did it and can do it again, you grow in confidence. You have the interest and intention to pursue your wealth building rather than playing by the middle rules and just getting by. What a different energy that carries with it!

There's an identity shift that comes with becoming an investor, and the more you commit to it, the more real your financial freedom becomes. It's no longer this far-off dream but rather something real and achievable.

You are normalising investing and wealth creation in your life, and that carries with it an incredible level of empowerment and momentum.

Again, it doesn't need to be a big step. Every journey begins with a baby step, and you are ready to take yours now. The very first step you need to take is to free up some cash to put into the market, so where might you find this first pot of gold?

Find your hidden treasures in the four types of money

Money can be classified into four different types:

- **Working money** (not to be confused with slave money) is out there working for you through your investments.
- **Slave money** is the money you earn in exchange for your time.

- **Safe money** is the money you have set aside to keep you safe so you can sleep soundly at night—for example, your personal buffers, insurances, metals as a hedge against a weak economy or currency, and savings.
- **Lazy money** is any money in your life that is not working as hard as it could be for you.

Want one big key to wealth building? Turn your lazy money into working money.

Let's look at some examples of lazy money that might be sitting in your life right now and that could be a hidden treasure for you just waiting for you to uncover it and put it to work.

Lazy money type 1: underutilised savings

People often think of money in the bank as 'safe' money. That may be true to an extent, depending of course on how much you trust the 'banksters'—I mean bankers—and the banking system.

However, there's a limit to what savings can do for you when they're simply sitting in cash. You are constrained by how much interest the banks are willing to pay you, which is usually not much; and if left to the ebb and flow of inflation, then you'll likely be going backwards. This is why cash is trash when it comes to wealth creation. Great for a little bit of protection and sound sleep, but you'll never save your way to wealth.

So decide what you need for your buffers and savings, then decide what savings you're not putting to good use. This could include excess emergency funds (beyond what's necessary), untouched savings for long-term goals that aren't being optimised or surplus cash you haven't allocated to any particular purpose.

While savings are important for financial security, you need to balance them with opportunities for growth. Don't let your savings sit idle; find a way to make that lazy money start working for you.

Lazy money type 2: wasted dollars

Wasted dollars are exactly what they sound like—money that has slipped through the cracks owing to inefficiencies in your financial habits. You've probably already spotted some during your 'plugging the leaks' exercise. It could be high-interest debt that's costing you a fortune, excessive fees, inefficient loan structures, unclaimed tax deductions, unnecessary expenses or those sneaky unused subscriptions that quietly drain your bank account every month.

By now you've likely identified some of these money-wasting habits and have a clearer picture of how much extra cashflow you could have each month once these leaks are plugged. So what do you do with that freed-up money? Here's a trick: a dollar without a plan and purpose will naturally flow towards low-value, low-priority activities. If you don't give that money a job, it will slowly evaporate from your life, leaving you wondering where it went.

Once you've uncovered these inefficiencies, the goal is to turn wasted dollars into working dollars by allocating this newly freed-up cash to something that will serve your long-term goals. It could be paying down other debt faster, building up your emergency fund or moving that money into investments that will generate higher returns. The key is to give every dollar a clear purpose, whether that's wealth building, debt reduction or strategic savings.

Lazy money type 3: untapped home equity

Let's talk about one of the biggest sources of lazy money: the untapped equity in your home. If you own property, you might have a treasure trove of potential wealth just sitting there, in the form of home equity, doing nothing. Now, I know many people love the idea of having a mortgage-free home or building up equity over time, but here's the thing: while that money is tied up in your property, it's not actively working to build more wealth for you.

Unlock your home equity

Your home equity is a dormant asset. It has value, but unless you tap into it that value is just sitting there. The good news is you can unlock this equity and put it to work without selling your home. Options like home equity loans, home equity lines of credit or refinancing allow you to access that money and use it strategically. Maybe it's to fund another investment, to start a business or even to make improvements to your current home that will increase its value.

Use equity wisely

Of course, tapping into your home equity comes with responsibility. You don't want to pull out this money for low-value purposes; after all you have to pay it back at some point. If you're going to be pulling equity out, it should be used for wealth-building activities—things that will give you a reliable return on your investment. Think of it as redeploying a lazy asset to something more productive. The goal is to make sure that, by leveraging your home's equity, you're putting yourself in a stronger financial position down the road.

Untapped home equity is one of the most common forms of lazy money. If it's just sitting there, you're missing out on opportunities to grow your wealth. The key is to unlock it responsibly and use it for investments or opportunities that will ultimately increase your financial standing.

I've seen many investors over the years access their equity and use it to rapidly grow their portfolios, from investing in real estate to deploying into high-income earning opportunities. It all comes down to a mathematical equation: If I can access x amount of equity at x per cent interest and use it to earn y per cent return, then is it a good deal or not? And is the return worth the risk?

Consider the flipside of this risk. What if you don't access your equity and get it working for you? What impact could that have on your financial results?

Lazy money type 4: poor-performing assets

If you have been investing for a while, then it's highly likely you have had that one investment—or maybe more than one—that just isn't pulling its weight. Whether it's a stock that's consistently underperforming, a piece of real estate that's not giving you the returns you hoped for or your retirement savings, these *poor-performing assets* are a classic example of lazy money. They're stuck in your portfolio, doing very little to help you achieve your financial goals.

Identify the dead weight

The first step in dealing with poor-performing assets is to recognise them. It's easy to hold onto an investment, hoping it will turn around or simply because you're emotionally attached to it. But here's the truth: sometimes you need to cut your losses. If an asset has been dragging its feet for too long, it's time to reassess whether it's worth holding onto or whether that money could be better used elsewhere.

Make the switch

Once you've identified these lazy assets, the goal is to replace them with something that offers better potential. It might be time to sell off that underperforming stock or reassess the value of your real estate holdings. The important part is making sure that every asset in your portfolio is actively contributing to your overall wealth-building strategy. Remember, your money should be working as hard as you are—don't let it stay lazy.

Right now you are just identifying opportunity; there is no need to do anything major just yet. You're dipping your toes in to get used to the temperature of the water. Now you need to decide what to do with all or some of it to get started.

Get started with micro-investing

Micro-investing, at its core, is simply investing small amounts of money at a time, so it's somewhere everyone can get started. It could be as little as five dollars. The point is to get started.

You might say, 'Well that's not going to get me far', and you'd be right. Micro-investing is just a starting point for a much bigger investing journey. But don't underestimate the impact of such a modest beginning. It increases your confidence and ensures you are personally and emotionally invested in the world of investing, meaning you align your unconscious mind towards the frequency of wealth building. And with the power of compounding, small amounts add up over time.

Also, it's fun—well, I find it fun anyway!

Again, you are normalising wealth building in your life, which means the bigger investments you make in the future aren't as daunting, as you have greater understanding, are more educated and aware, and so much more.

So how do you actually make it happen? Let's lay it out step by step.

First, get clear on how much and how often you can contribute towards your micro-investing strategy. Now set this up in your freedom account so it is prioritised for this purpose only.

Next, decide what assets you'd like to start building towards. There are generally only limited options with small capital levels, but more than enough to get going with. Shares and equities, cryptocurrencies and micro-investing in pools, or metals such as gold and silver, are commonly accessible.

I talk to many of my investors just starting out about the *investment trifecta*. These are three micro-investment opportunities:

- **metals such as gold and silver**—not only a potential growth asset but a possible hedge against a weak economy
- **shares, equities, funds**—another potential growth asset, but offering the potential to earn dividends
- **cryptocurrencies**—a potential high-growth asset class, digital currencies are the future, so you need to get a holding in them.

Here's why I love this classification:

- You are hitting three different strategies—buy and hold, paycheque and momentum (more on this in the next chapter).
- You are diversifying across three different asset classes.
- You have the capacity to diversify across different jurisdictions.
- Each of these classes is usually very liquid if required.

Research platforms

Don't just choose the first random option that comes your way. Put your investor hat on and do some research. Criteria for how to choose the best investing platforms include:

- established and reputable offerings, and companies with a solid track record
- easy and convenient entry and exit, meaning you can get your money in and out easily and quickly
- low minimum investment amount—some platforms have a minimum investment amount; make sure your investment capacity fits
- ability to automate your investments—so you can set it on autopilot, allowing you to make automatic contributions through either rounding up your purchases or setting up recurring deposits
- tracking and reporting is clear and transparent—so you can monitor your investments
- regulation—should the platform be regulated, and Is it?
- reputation—what are other people saying about it? Check out reviews and feedback.
- mobile apps—it's convenient to be able to review and increase your holdings from your phone.
- low fees—especially when you might be investing small amounts, you want to be sure the platform isn't chewing up your returns in fees.
- security—make sure the platform takes its security very seriously.
- support—you want to be able to reach someone when you really need to.
- user-friendly—a good micro-investing platform should be easy to navigate and user-friendly. The app or website

should have a simple interface that makes it easy to track your investments, monitor performance and make changes.

Once you've decided on your platform, you will need to:

- *set your rhythms*. How often and how much are you going to invest in which opportunity? Set something specific and manageable so you make sure you are setting yourself up to the win in the game of money and wealth building.
- *automate it*. I won't say set and forget, because you'll be reviewing your portfolio regularly, but if you can automate the onboarding of your capital in the opportunity, it makes it even more convenient and also removes human error.
- *add to your weekly money night reviews*. Finally, add the review of this portfolio to your money night. Check in on it and track your inputs and performance regularly, and keep on normalising wealth creation in your life as you watch your portfolio begin to grow.

Some might ask if micro-investing is relevant for them, given that they are already experienced investors. Well, if it holds any weight for you, I still do it! If you haven't got the message already, I cannot stand lazy money in my portfolio. I will always get it out there and working for me, no matter how small it is. Although I may have solid bases in each of the asset classes I invest in, I still do dollar-cost averaging regularly as I keep building these elements of my portfolio.

Make wealth building fun

Whenever I go shopping with my daughter, she knows the coconut water aisle is one of my regulars. Annabelle is always hoping I don't find what I'm looking for, which is a '50 per cent off' sale on the coconut water I like. Because then I don't just get one or two bottles.

I tend to go a bit overboard and load up my trolley—I'm talking 20 or even 40 bottles. Let's just say she finds it a little embarrassing when I'm skipping down the aisles with my extravagant haul of coconut water, looking pleased with myself.

I'm still grinning like a jackal when we hit the register. One of the fun money games I play with myself is around how much I can save and invest in a single shop. So once I get the receipt and see how much I saved from intelligent shopping, I'm onto my investment apps and investing those babies instantly. Two minutes later my money is invested, I have my coconut water, I've embarrassed my daughter (again) and I'm a happy camper.

Now, you may read this and be saying to yourself, *there's something wrong with this guy*, and you may be right, but that little money game I play has made me some decent coin over time. It's also fun, and my competitive nature loves it.

Maybe this isn't your game, but perhaps you have others. The point is to have fun with your wealth building. You're taking control of your financial life and creating freedom for yourself and your loved ones. Why not enjoy the process, and remember that the more you interact with money, the more money will interact with you. So try gamifying your wealth building: set challenges, make up games, and be constantly filling your interactions with money and wealth building with them good vibes.

Above all else, just get started. Remember, micro-investing is not the end, it is only the beginning, and even if you are an experienced investor already, never underestimate the power of compounding on your wealth-building journey.

Power points

- If you don't get your money working hard for you, you'll spend your entire life just working hard for money—and stuck in the middle.

- Shift your normal. For most people, normal is working their entire lives just to pay the bills. Why not normalise wealth creation and financial freedom instead?

- There's an identity shift that comes with becoming an investor, and the more you commit to it, the more real your financial freedom becomes.

- The four types of money:

  1. Working money is money that is working for you.

  2. Slave money is money you earn by working.

  3. Safe money is money you have set aside to keep you safe.

  4. Lazy money is money in your life that is not working as hard as it could be.

- A big key to wealth building is turning your lazy money into working money.

- The four major types of lazy money are:

  - underutilised savings

  - wasted dollars

  - untapped home equity

  - poor-performing assets.

- Micro-investing is simply investing small amounts of money at a time.

- Micro-investing is the first step in a larger investment journey. Don't underestimate its impact—it builds confidence and engages you personally and emotionally, aligning your mindset with the path to wealth building.

CHAPTER 14

THE FULL CIRCLE STRATEGY

An investor whose 'strategy' relies solely on deciding what property or share or crypto coin to buy is missing most of the game.

We need to come back to what the big goal is when we start out on the journey of creating financial freedom. Remember, it isn't to buy a bunch of assets; it's to establish a proven wealth system that allows you to grow a sustainable diversified portfolio of quality assets that delivers a consistent and reliable income stream into your bank account to fund the lifestyle you desire.

So what we do must run far deeper than the assets themselves. In fact, when you are crafting your system you are utilising seven different strategies. I call this the *full circle strategy* (see figure 14.1, overleaf).

The full circle strategy

Full circle brings together seven different pillars of your financial life that, working in harmony, help you move towards creating your financial freedom figure and taking back your freedom.

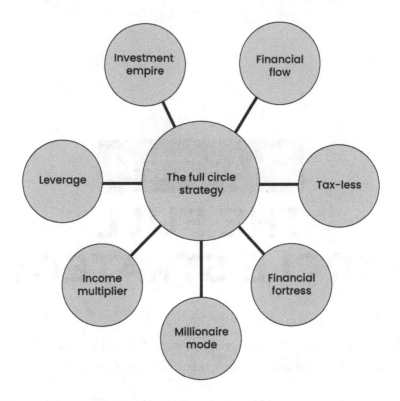

Figure 14.1: the full circle strategy

Going full circle creates a snowball effect in your portfolio. One layer of strategy is stacked on top of another and another, until the momentum becomes unstoppable.

These are the seven strategies:

1. Finance farm

This is where you plug the financial leaks in your money bucket, plan where each dollar goes and automate it so it doesn't require your daily input.

> *The efficiency factor:* It's not about how much you make, it's what you do with what you make that makes the difference.

2. Tax-less

When I talk about taxes, I'm not only describing the system you need for legally reducing the tax you pay to the government. I'm also referring to what author and business mentor Keith Cunningham, in his book the *Road Less Stupid*, calls 'dumb tax'. A dumb tax is any tax you pay because of making inefficient—or, frankly, dumb—decisions that cost you money, time, lost opportunity and a heck of an amount of stress.

> The *intelligence* factor: Financial success comes from better financial decision making.

3. Financial fortress

This is the system to keep you, your family and your portfolio safe. It involves having your strategic personal and investment buffers in place, ensuring your portfolio is set up in the right asset-protection vehicles, and having a plan for strategically locking away and securing your wealth over time.

> *The longevity factor:* Investing success is not only about how much you make; it's about how much you keep.

4. Millionaire mode

This is your personal system for stepping up. If you want to raise your results, then you have to raise the standards of how you are showing up. The most valuable piece of real estate any of us owns is the one between our ears—our minds. Unless this critical element is handled, all the education, the strategy, the tools and the deals won't be implemented at the level they need to be to create the results you want.

> *The mastery factor:* You will never out-earn yourself.

5. Income multiplier

This is the system for creating multiple income streams. Relying on one income stream is risky and a slow way to build wealth. Three income streams are the benchmark for creating a good income and, as with anything else, there's a system to create them. I call it the *income freedom formula*. It is a step-by-step process of moving from 'active' to 'passive' income streams.

> *The accelerator factor:* Raising your investable income and applying it to a well-crafted wealth strategy can accelerate your wealth journey more than almost any other action.

6. The six levers of leverage

If your success is based only on your own resources of time, money, experience, energy and knowledge, your results will always be limited. Effectively, you become the bottleneck to your own success. The six levers of leverage are as follows:

1. **You.** Double down and tap into your own unique strengths rather than focusing only on your weaknesses.
2. **Knowledge.** Learn from mentors, tapping into their expertise and experience.
3. **People.** Build a world-class team to help guide you and execute your wealth-building plans.
4. **Financial.** Utilise other people's money (OPM), such as bank lending, so you aren't limited by your own financial resources (particularly important for property investing).
5. **Network.** Leverage other people's networks and relationships to open doors to opportunities.
6. **Systems.** Follow systems that deliver predictable results, so you're not constantly reinventing the wheel.

The constraint factor: Learn to identify the biggest roadblocks on your wealth-building journey and seek the solutions to move past them by tapping into resources well beyond your own.

7. The asset accelerator

This is the system for choosing what wealth vehicles you will add into your portfolio and, more importantly, what purpose they will serve to help you move from one phase of your portfolio to the next.

The purpose factor: It's not about the deal, it's about the purpose the deal serves in your portfolio.

In this chapter I zero in on the seventh of these strategies—the *asset accelerator.* To truly understand this, we first need to redefine what an asset actually is.

In the world of investing, an asset is usually considered something that can be exchanged for cash, be it property, shares, crypto or something else. This is a limited view of the true potential of an asset.

I define an asset as 'an owned resource that has the potential to generate future economic value'.

Economic value could relate to:

- an asset as a source of value—anything of value that can generate income or future benefit, or be exchanged for other resources
- ownership and control—something owned or controlled by a person or entity, whether it's tangible (such as property) or intangible (such as patents)
- economic benefit—with the expectation that the asset will deliver positive economic value directly or indirectly.

The key takeaways across all these definitions are ownership, control, value and the potential for economic benefit. This is at the core of understanding what wealthy people do differently.

The wealthy build assets through their earning ability; the structures they set up to own or control their investment assets and business; the systems they leverage off, which do the heavy lifting for them, create predictable results and fast-track their progress; and the investment assets they accumulate to create cashflow and value.

The asset accelerator

Every investor requires three different asset types within their portfolio as they construct their system. Miss one and things can come to a grinding halt, as they do in so many investors' portfolios.

The asset accelerator is the strategic framework I use when working with investors to help them choose the individual assets they are going to begin accumulating, based on their personal strategy, and how to combine them to form a cohesive system that delivers real-world results.

The overarching premise of this framework is that strategy is not about the asset class itself; rather, it's about the purpose it serves in the portfolio.

Read that again to make sure you grasp the concept. We're not going to get caught up in whether it's property or shares or crypto or metals or lending or joint ventures or business or whisky or rare coins or art or anything else you might think of. All of them may in fact serve a purpose within a portfolio, but we choose them later.

Strategy first, deals second.

I'm going to walk you through each of these portfolio assets one by one. I'll be using property as an example, for no reason other than it is easy to understand.

Strategy 1. 'Buy and gold'

Primary purpose: capital growth

Uses:

- to create equity value in assets, which can then be leveraged off to access more capital to acquire additional assets
- to store wealth as part of your financial freedom portfolio. I use the term 'buy and gold' when describing this asset type because of the intrinsic value it holds within the portfolio and of the core purpose it serves within your financial freedom portfolio: storing wealth. This asset forms the foundation for generating a consistent, sustainable income stream to support the lifestyle you envision.
- to safeguard against economic downturns. These assets often perform better in challenging times, as their inherent desirability can create a unique market demand. Gold and silver, for example, serve as safe-haven investments and typically increase in value under such conditions.

Limitations: the cost of the asset itself, which requires more upfront capital and lower potential yields, meaning lower cashflow

Asset classes: blue-chip property (both residential and commercial); blue-chip shares; major cryptocurrencies such as Bitcoin and Ethereum; gold and silver; blue-chip managed funds and indexes; private equity positions in businesses; artworks and more.

A closer look at residential property

When it comes to property investing, the buy-and-gold assets are your blue-chip properties—better properties in better locations that are more desirable for people to live in.

Their desirability means these properties tend to outperform the rest of the market in terms of capital growth—they are an 'equity escalator', driving up the value of your asset base. This is the primary purpose of the buy-and-gold asset type, and the growth in the value of the assets you hold is where your true wealth is going to be created.

For the type of portfolio where you want to hold your wealth and receive an income that is consistent, sustainable and reliable enough for you to hang your freedom hat on, many investors choose the buy-and-gold asset type.

Every asset type has its limitations, though. In property, because these properties are in higher demand, the cost of getting involved is often a heck of a lot higher, requiring more capital out of your pocket.

The yields can also be a lot lower, and in the world of property and lending, if you have a big loan on this style of property, you can end up negatively geared and bleeding cashflow.

I'll make a point on negative gearing in property investing. I never have a problem with a negatively geared property. Some of my best deals have been negatively geared, as they earned me hundreds of thousands, even millions, in capital growth. I do have a problem with a negatively geared portfolio, however. The point is to never get caught up in the individual deal; keep your focus on what purpose this deal is serving in your overall portfolio system.

Back to buy-and-gold portfolio building. I've seen many investors attempt to focus on this pathway and this pathway alone, only to find they get stuck after running out of capital, running low on cashflow and using up all their lending capacity with the banks. Frustrated, they're waiting for their income and values to catch up so they can eventually (hopefully) start moving forward again. This can differ from country to country depending on the local finance and property markets.

One of my clients, Heather, found herself in just this situation. Heather had built a $10.7 million property portfolio in Australia. Her properties were amazing. The growth had been incredible and her net asset value was strong, at over $5 million. She had achieved what very few people have and was a multi-millionaire. The only problem? Heather was stuck—stuck with lending, stuck with cashflow as the portfolio was only yielding $5597 per year, stuck in her portfolio and still stuck in a job despite the value of her assets.

What was missing? Well, the other two asset types of course.

The first step for Heather was to create liquidity, as she had no hope of getting any further lending from the banks. We assessed her current portfolio and chose three of the properties we felt had plateaued and were no longer an essential part of her financial freedom portfolio to trade back to the market. (Similar to the negative gearing conversation, I never get caught up in buy-and-hold or buy-and-sell in investing; I only get caught up in doing whatever the hell works.)

After realising this capital, we began to diversify into the other two strategy types.

Strategy 2: Paycheque

Primary purpose: consistent cashflow

Uses:

- *Portfolio cashflow.* Ensure your portfolio is always positive cashflow, putting money in your back pocket and not bleeding you dry.
- *Servicing.* Depending on the asset type, consistency and length of time holding the asset, these asset styles may help support your servicing with lenders in order to access more lending to leverage into more opportunities.
- *Capital accumulation.* As you grow your cashflow, you can build up more savings to fund further asset accumulation and begin compounding your portfolio.
- *Debt reduction.* Depending on what stage you are in and the needs of your portfolio at this time, you may direct the excess cashflow towards debt reduction, thereby reducing debt, increasing income and increasing servicing.

Limitations: Depending on the asset class, higher yielding assets may attract lower levels of capital growth. Or rather than it being a tangible asset, such as property, you might deploy lending or high-income strategies, which I consider tactics rather than assets given they have a start and stop time and you have rights only to the income stream generated for a period of time.

Asset classes: commercial properties, multi-family properties, rooming houses, high-yielding shares, private equity, lending opportunities, loan notes, yield plays and staking in cryptocurrencies, consistent trading results and internet businesses, to name a few.

Most people get their cashflow exclusively from their job or business. This is always going to be a limiting factor within the portfolio. If you rely on only this income when trying to accumulate assets in your portfolio, your capital, cashflow, lending capacity with banks and ability to eliminate debt will all be limited.

Relying on one income stream is incredibly risky, as I have suggested. Remember, two income streams is okay, three is stable, and over and above that you move into the world of abundance.

What sets these types of income streams apart comes down to consistency. If you are earning income, yet the returns are inconsistent, then you will allocate this style of asset to the Momentum quadrant, which we will talk about next. What we want is reliability and to establish a 'cashflow cascade' in your portfolio. This creates an asset that you can then predictably deploy in other areas of the portfolio to move past obstacles, access opportunities and cashflow assets, create choices and so much more.

Back to Heather. As I've seen in many established investors' portfolios, she was asset rich and cashflow poor. The asset base is beautiful but if it's not giving you the desired choices in life, then what's the point? The first big move we needed to make in Heather's portfolio was to establish some consistent income streams. This would ensure the portfolio was not only taking care of itself but beginning to deliver some well-overdue cashflow back into Heather's back pocket.

Next was to begin to support the build-up of Heather's capital base to deploy into more paycheque and momentum opportunities. Ultimately, this would facilitate the transition of Heather's portfolio towards a system that delivers consistent income. So far she has deployed into three paycheque opportunities, with returns of 20 per cent, 25 per cent and 15 per cent per annum, bringing in a total of $69 000—and we're just getting started.

Strategy 3. Momentum

Primary purpose: realised profits

Uses: Momentum strategies are designed to turn over chunks of profit. You then get the choice of what to do with the profits you create:

- *Portfolio cashflow.* Momentum strategies can facilitate ensuring your portfolio is cashflow positive; however, often the profits you gain from these assets are erratic and inconsistent. With the right mix and the right liquidity points you can certainly establish this, but it takes careful planning and diversification of opportunities.
- *Redeploy profits.* Direct them into buy-and-gold asset accumulation using larger chunks of capital, which can result in lower leverage required if buying property or in higher buying capacity in other asset classes.
- *Capital accumulation.* Build up your available capital to deploy into further paycheque or momentum strategies, compounding your deployed capital and raising your potential returns and diversity of returns.
- *Debt reduction.* These profit chunks, if allocated wisely, will pay down the debt on your portfolio far faster than any principle-and-interest loan from the bank. Remember Jim Rohn's advice: profits are better than wages. Use these profits to pay down your debt in rapid chunks.

Limitations: This asset style is often used for a trading asset, meaning you deploy your capital into a deal or lending tactic or business opportunity for a period of time, depending on the opportunity. But your outcome is to get your principle plus profits back out ready to decide where to deploy them next. This means it's a more active strategy that requires you to then find more opportunities to redeploy to, and you don't physically own an asset for a holding spot in the portfolio over the long term. In this instance, it is an acceleration tool for the rest of your portfolio.

Asset classes: Flipping, trading, some cryptocurrencies, joint ventures and business investments are examples.

The momentum asset is a trading asset, whether trading in and out of the market on a daily basis in the cryptocurrency or share market, or flipping real estate over a six- to 12-month period from a subdivision or renovation/refurb or strata title, or investing in a business closing in on an exit in the next three to five years. Whatever the hold timeline ends up being, this is not a 'buy and hold forever'. At the end of the day, your asset may be gone, but you have the capital to show for it.

I talk to my clients about setting up what I call a 'profit pipeline', which means setting it so a regular chunk of profits flows back into your life every one to two years. This gives you the opportunity to redeploy your capital towards the highest and best use within your portfolio at each decision point, whether it be to pay down debt in big chunks or to grow the capital base you are deploying across paycheque or momentum deals to compound your returns or to build a bigger deposit to migrate back into more blue-chip opportunities.

This was another key missing piece for Heather. The core assets were there, but there remained a 50 per cent loan-to-value ratio (LVR) of debt on them. Coupled with some low yields from the assets and no servicing, the portfolio was at a standstill. What would help it break free from its stagnation and turn the portfolio from not just being asset rich but being cashflow rich? Establishing a strong profit pipeline and compounding it, growing the capital being deployed and using the profits—after three years of compounding—to begin destroying the remaining debt.

Heather has deployed into five momentum opportunities so far. These were a mix of joint ventures and business deals, and if they all play out as planned will earn Heather $552 000 in profit over the next three years with two additional, higher risk, higher reward style opportunities to cash in as they mature.

Going from only $5597 in cashflow from a $10 million-plus portfolio to $69 000 in the first 12 months, and setting up profit returns of over $500 000 to drip in over the following three years and beyond from diverse opportunities, demonstrates how valuable establishing a comprehensive system in your portfolio is. Heather now has a targeted system to reactivate her portfolio and realise her dreams of financial freedom.

Three years to financially free—that's the plan in play.

Each of the asset types has benefits and drawbacks. Many people try to hunt unicorn deals that have high capital growth, high cashflow, high liquidity and high security—and wind up turning down a multitude of great deals in their search for the perfect one. If you find the fabled field of lost unicorn deals, make sure you let me know and we can go rescue some together.

So how do you choose which of the three strategies is right for you? And what is your next move? Here are the principal factors to consider:

- liquid capital
- borrowing capacity with the banks
- untapped equity
- savings ability
- income levels
- debt levels
- future earning capacity
- age
- risk profile
- experience
- investable income
- buying power
- portfolio income.

Consider whether these are high or low, accessible or inaccessible, risky or conservative, diverse or concentrated when choosing what to do next.

It's not enough just to think about what you need to do to get into another deal. You should be looking ahead to begin setting up elements that will help you move towards your financial freedom goal faster.

There's a great series on Netflix called *The Queen's Gambit* about a young chess prodigy named Beth who was orphaned and learned how to play chess from the maintenance guy at the orphanage. Two scenes show Beth playing chess games in her mind.

The first is when she is a young girl who has fallen in love with the game of chess and is beginning to master moves and countermoves.

As she is lying in her dormitory bed, while all the girls around her are sleeping, Beth is staring at the ceiling where a massive upside-down chess board floats. We watch both black and white moves and countermoves as the game is played out.

The second scene is in the middle of a chess tournament. Beth closes her eyes and when she opens them again the chess game is playing out in front of her. Again, we watch what is going on in her mind as she runs through all her moves and the countermoves of her opponent until the inevitable checkmate—and the game is hers.

Beth's ability to see many moves in advance sees her win many matches, culminating in her becoming the first woman to win the world chess championship in Russia at an incredibly young age.

They say a chess grandmaster can see 17 moves ahead in their game, including all moves and countermoves. We need to think the same way when it comes to investing. Thinking about the next deal is not enough. We need to look multiple moves ahead to ensure the decisions we make now are not just about progressing on the board to take another pawn, but contribute to our being able to declare, a few moves later, 'Checkmate' to the middle and take back our freedom.

So here are a few questions to ask yourself:

Where is the greatest opportunity you have yet to tap into? (Think untapped equity, high servicing levels, high savings capacity and so on.)

Is there a clear, long-term opportunity in your situation that will help accelerate your portfolio overall? (Think high levels of servicing due to higher and expanding incomes, high savings capacity, cash windfalls or equity growth.)

What is the biggest limiting factor in your portfolio right now? (Servicing, cashflow, capital?)

What do you feel will be the biggest limiting factor in your portfolio over the longer term? (Servicing, timeline of working life, income, cashflow?)

I warned you this chapter was a step up from the previous. We're now deep in the world of wealth building and at every level there's another devil to understand. So give yourself a round of applause for being prepared to get real with yourself and your portfolio and make your financial freedom a priority.

Now you have the tools to build your strategy, it's implementation time. How do you find the deals that will make more profit and cashflow to accelerate your journey?

Power points

- If you don't get your money working hard for you, you'll spend your entire life just working hard for money—and stuck in the middle.

- Shift your normal. For most people, normal is working their entire lives just to pay the bills. Why not normalise wealth creation and financial freedom instead?

- There's an identity shift that comes with becoming an investor, and the more you commit to it, the more real your financial freedom becomes.

- The four types of money:

  - Working money is money that is working for you.

  - Slave money is money you earn by working.

  - Safe money is money you have set aside to keep you safe.

  - Lazy money is money in your life that is not working as hard as it could be.

- A big key to wealth building is turning your lazy money into working money.

- The four types of lazy money are:

  - underutilised savings

  - wasted dollars

  - untapped home equity

  - poor-performing assets.

- Micro-investing is simply investing small amounts of money at a time.

- Micro-investing is the first step in a larger investment journey. Don't underestimate its impact—it builds confidence and engages you personally and emotionally, aligning your mindset with the path to wealth building.

CHAPTER 15

FIND THE DEALS THAT MAKE THE DIFFERENCE

The most beautifully laid out and shrewdly structured strategy in the world means squat unless you find the deals that make the difference in your portfolio. Average deals bring average results and a portfolio that feels stagnant or lazy, and no one has time for that.

I'm not talking about your run-of-the-mill investment in shares on the ASX or the S&P 500 or a property on the real estate sourcing sites. Some of these might turn out great, but the real opportunities that consistently accelerate and transform your financial life are found elsewhere.

These are the off-market deals that are snapped up well before they ever reach the mainstream. It's like the difference between shopping wholesale versus retail.

Don't be a seagull

Imagine you are at the beach enjoying some fresh fish and chips. You're sitting there enjoying the view, watching the people, and the seagulls crowd in, waiting expectantly.

Then you accidentally knock a chip off the picnic table—and time freezes.

The chip begins to fall, as if in slow motion, and as it does so a shadow passes over the table as a hundred seagulls, locked on to that chip, descend in a whirlwind of feathery chaos. One gull snatches and swallows it in the blink of an eye and the chaos settles, the seagulls returning to their waiting game.

Now maybe deal hunting isn't as dramatic as this, but it's definitely what on-market deal hunting can be like in a hot deal.

I'm writing this chapter in Singapore. My wife, Nerissa, and I spent yesterday looking at property here. The first place we went to felt like the first chip had fallen. It was a grand opening and, well, the developer's marketing department did their job. It was chaos, aggressive seagulls everywhere, making it hard to move around, and a ticketing system in play just to view the display suite. The property had some unique features, but it just wasn't standing out for us. What's more, a ballot system was required to register your interest and decide if you were privileged enough even to get a chance to purchase—not my preferred method of buying deals, that's for sure, so we left.

Immediately afterwards we went to another development. This was in a super-prime location and was built by a more prestigious developer known for their ultra-luxury developments. Living there would be like coming home to a six-star hotel designed like an art gallery. Nerissa's agent, with whom she had built up a relationship over a number of years, had introduced us to the opportunity. This off-market opportunity was not listed on the standard property search sites so there was no swarm of people to push through; the whole event was wonderfully calm, even serene. Something had shifted in the market and the developer needed to sell their final pieces so they could move on to another project. There was a deal to be done.

We made an offer to purchase this property, including a 12-month deferred settlement with the ability to move in earlier and a solid discount off the asking price, and right now we're waiting for the negotiations to begin or, even better, acceptance.

It's a cracker.

Now let me introduce you to the Deal Flow System (see figure 15.1), a streamlined process designed to help you find, analyse and execute high-quality off-market deals. Once secured, you can integrate these deals into your portfolio seamlessly, ensuring they operate smoothly so you can confidently re-enter the market and keep growing your investments.

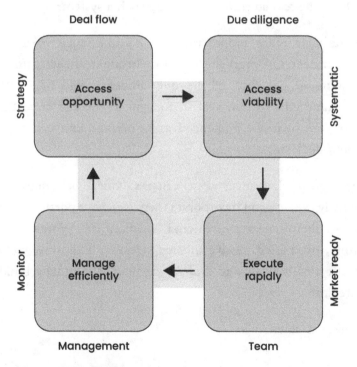

Figure 15.1: the deal flow system

As you can see, there are four key elements to consider:

1. **Access opportunity.** How do you get access to off-market deals to begin with?
2. **Assess viability.** How do you conduct rapid, top-level due diligence on a deal to get to a strong YES or a strong NO?
3. **Execute rapidly.** Once you have a deal, how do you secure it and execute on it quickly and safely?
4. **Manage efficiently.** Install the deal in your portfolio, freeing you up to go back and hunt for more.

One reason why so many investors choose to work with me and the Portfolio group of companies is because my Deal Flow System is highly effective; after all, I've spent more than 20 years refining it.

But what's the real advantage of having such a system?

With the right team supporting you, it's like receiving a silver-plated service. Off-market deals are brought directly to your desk, with 90 per cent of the due diligence and negotiations already handled. All that's left is for you to run the opportunity through your own due diligence framework and arrive at a quick, confident decision.

For the deals that meet your criteria, you'll be equipped to confidently execute and incorporate them into your portfolio. These deals can then generate additional cashflow and profits, leading to strong, diversified passive income streams. This way, you can move effortlessly from one deal to the next, continually building your wealth.

Let's break it down.

Step 1. Access opportunity

When it comes to finding 'off-market' deals, there are two ways to approach it: you can follow a do-it-yourself approach where you go and build the deal pipeline yourself, or you can join a network that has a pipeline already established. There's no right or wrong option; it comes down to what's right for you.

Some people love nothing more than researching markets and finding investments to do due diligence on. Others would rather stab themselves with something sharp than do all that work.

In my experience, most people are busy enough in life with work, family and living and prefer to tap into a 'done-for-you' system than develop one themselves.

Whichever path you choose, what's important to understand is that it's less about *what* you know and more about *who* you know. Technical knowledge is certainly important in some instances, but getting access comes from building long-term relationships based on trust and performance. This is, of course, something that can be developed over time if you so desire, but be prepared to put in the time and patience it will require.

Here are some of the places where investors go hunting to find off-market investment opportunities:

- **Networking**. Build relationships with brokers, real estate agents and other investors. Industry events and professional organisations are great places to connect with insiders.
- **Direct outreach**. Reach out directly to property or business owners who haven't listed their assets yet. A well-timed letter, email or call could land you an exclusive deal.

- **Private equity and investment clubs**. Join private equity firms or investment clubs where off-market opportunities are shared within the group.
- **Professional advisers**. Leverage accountants, lawyers and financial planners who might know about discreet sales before they hit the market.
- **Social media**. Use LinkedIn and niche online platforms to connect with sellers and find off-market opportunities.
- **Reputation**. Build your credibility as a reliable investor, and more deals will come your way.
- **Market research**. Stay ahead by researching local markets, economic trends and distressed assets before they go public.

Your job is to build trust and relationships and begin to get in on the inner circle of these opportunities, or if you are intending to do the deals yourself, develop your market knowledge so you actually know a deal when you find one.

Step 2. Assess viability

Once you have an opportunity on the table, you need to be able to assess that deal to see if it's a fit for you and your situation. This is where doing effective due diligence comes into play. You run the deal through a strategic due diligence framework to arrive at a strong 'Yes, I want to explore further,' or maybe a strong 'No, this deal is not for me.'

The importance of reaching a strong yes or no quickly cannot be overstated. Great deals often move fast, and you have to be prepared to act quickly. Remember that property in Singapore Nerissa and

I put in an offer for? Because of the nature of the deal, we had less than 24 hours to finalise our due diligence and get to a decision. In this case it was a go-ahead deal for us; our offer was in and I'm writing this 24 hours later: our offer was negotiated within the day and accepted with all the terms we wanted. We were told that we were the only ones in the entire development to have landed the deal on these terms.

If we had taken two weeks to come back to them, we wouldn't have had a chance, and the deal would have been taken elsewhere.

One point that needs repeating goes back to the third habit of millionaire investors, personal responsibility. No matter how much due diligence is done on your behalf by a deal provider, when you step onto the field to decide if this deal is right for you or not, you take on the responsibility for your choice. It's up to you to dot the i's and cross the t's wherever you choose to invest your money and then to take full responsibility for your decision.

Returning to the due diligence framework, as shown in figure 15.2, there are four levels of due diligence you need to address when assessing an opportunity.

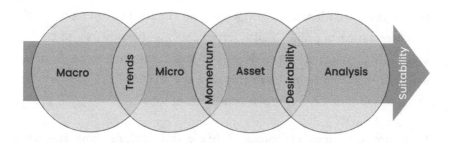

Figure 15.2: the four levels of due diligence

Level #1: macro

At the macro level of due diligence, what you are trying to ascertain is the potential big-picture trends in the location, country, region or even the world. These are trends that generally impact everyone, such as:

- economic growth and stability—monetary policy, interest rate movements, inflation or confidence, for example
- technological advancement—such as the impact of AI and blockchain
- demographic shifts—such as ageing population, influence of different generations
- environmental and social governance—consider climate change and sustainability
- geopolitical factors—trade policies, supply chains, international relations and the political landscape
- consumer behaviour and preferences—e-commerce versus retail, increased focus on health, wellness and longevity
- regulatory environment—such as blockchain and cryptocurrency regulation, central bank digital currencies, tax reforms
- emergency situations—such as public health crises or wars.

Is the deal you are considering aligned with some of the bigger trends you have identified, and what does that mean for its potential success? Think of public health issues causing lockdowns and travel bans; office space investment versus shifts towards more flexible working environments; traditional ways of business versus the expectation that AI will replace millions of jobs.

In a property market context, this could include how interest rates impact lending and affordability, how government policies impact the rental market or the property supply pipeline, or how environmental considerations are changing energy efficiency requirements in property.

These macro trends interact in complex ways, shaping the investment landscape and presenting both challenges and opportunities for investors.

Level #2: micro

The micro layer of your due diligence funnel is about understanding specific, sector-focused and short-term factors that can influence investment decisions and market momentum.

These could include:

- economic microtrends, such as the availability of credit and lending standards, and how they might impact how much lending people may be able to get
- supply and demand imbalances, and how these drive demand in an area or sector
- local population growth
- demographic microtrends, such as downsizing
- infrastructure planning, the impact on government or institutional investment, and creating more desirable places for people to live
- regulatory changes in local areas, such as certain blockchain projects being considered unlicensed securities.

An example of this in the property world is using the PIE principle to assess the momentum or potential momentum of an area. PIE stands for:

- **p**opulation growth—how this drives demand in the area
- **i**nfrastructure—how this increases desirability for people
- **e**mployment nodes—how this impacts socioeconomics and affordability.

All these together indicate that it is a desirable place to live now and potentially it will be an even more desirable place in the future, attracting greater demand, which in turn pushes prices higher.

Level #3: asset

One layer deeper, and we're now conducting due diligence on the asset itself. Again using property as an example, consider that you have done your macro level of due diligence and have concluded that the property market is still ripe for growth or cashflow returns.

You've zeroed in on an area or set of suburbs that are showing signs of momentum in the market. Now it's time to choose the property itself and do the due diligence to ensure it has the potential to outperform the rest of the market.

Personally, I like to invest in property that effectively creates its own economy, meaning its desirable features will always be in strong demand by buyers or renters alike. These types of properties are less impacted by the ups and downs of the economy and market and tend to outperform.

Other things to consider are, to name a few, design and layout, ensuring the floor plan is functional and desirable, with an aesthetic appeal for the local demographic; the quality of materials and craftsmanship; energy efficiency; neighbourhood appeal; and proximity to parks and lifestyle infrastructure.

To read more, head over to www.escapethemiddle.com/guides for a comprehensive property investor due diligence pack.

For a *business* investment, I would now be evaluating the founder and their experience, looking at the competitive advantage of the business itself, assessing the quality of the brand, the depth of their business moat, the product-to-market fit and more.

If I were investing in *crypto*, I'd be assessing the business behind the coin and its use case. I'd be going through the white paper and seeking to understand the team. And I'd be getting clear on the roadmap.

If I were putting capital into a property joint venture or private lending opportunity, I'd be assessing the developer and builder and their experience and past projects, and if their planned product, whether it be houses, townhouses or units, was desirable in the area. I would also want to know what security is being offered and what the risk elements are.

Here we are zeroing in on the asset itself and making sure it is a desirable product to the market no matter what its asset class.

Level #4: analysis

The final level of due diligence is analysis, and is all about the numbers. Your job at this level is to make sure all the numbers make sense with regard to the asset cashflow, tax benefits, risk-to-reward ratio and projections, if relevant.

You're making sure the final boxes are ticked, the final sums are understood and everything is in place to ensure you can slide that baby right into your portfolio, and it is going to help and not hinder your progress towards living your dream lifestyle.

Once the deal has passed through this funnel, you're positioned to give a strong confirmation that you will proceed to the next level.

Step 3. Execute rapidly

So you've completed your due diligence and decided to go for it. Now what? It's time to secure and settle the deal safely and effectively.

This is certainly no time to take your foot off the pedal. You must take careful, methodical action that maintains your forward momentum, ensuring you're staying safe and communicating fully with the other parties, so everyone is on the same page and you are building a relationship as a good person to do business with.

There are three things to be mindful of in this phase:

- negotiating terms—putting together a win–win deal with the vendor
- securing the deal—taking the deal off the market
- managing emotions—continuing to make decisions based on facts and due diligence.

Negotiating terms

It's likely you were presented with some terms when the initial opportunity was brought to you. Sometimes those terms are hard and immovable, and you must decide whether or not they are acceptable to you. At other times the terms are negotiable, and you have the opportunity to structure something more advantageous to you and to the deal provider.

Here's a list of terms used when negotiating investment opportunities:

- *purchase price*—often flexible based on other conditions in the deal
- *financing terms*—including interest rates, down payment requirements, payment schedules or seller financing options
- *equity stake*—the percentage of ownership or profits each party receives
- *profit split*—how profits will be divided between the parties after certain returns are met

- *exit strategy*—terms related to when and how the investment will be exited, including buyout options, sale timeline or IPO terms
- *risk mitigation*—conditions for protecting against losses, such as performance guarantees, insurance or hedging strategies
- *management control*—deciding who has control over daily operations or decision making, or key roles in the management team
- *operational roles*—deciding who handles what responsibilities in managing the investment or property
- *capital contributions*—the amount each party will invest initially and in the future if more capital is needed
- *investment time horizon*—the length of time the investor or partner is expected to hold the investment before an exit
- *tax considerations*—negotiating how tax benefits or liabilities will be shared or structured
- *closing date*—the timeline for finalising the deal, which can be shifted for mutual benefit
- *due diligence period*—length of time allowed for reviewing financials, legal matters and conducting property inspections before committing to the deal
- *early access*—gaining early access to an opportunity while it is under contract but not yet settled to begin conducting works on an asset
- *yields*—regular cashflow distributions received through part ownership or cashflow distribution rights
- *timeline of distributions*—frequency of cashflow or profit distributions paid out to you
- *security*—amount and quality of security an investor will receive or can access in the case of a breach of agreement or non-performance.

This is a solid starting list but there are potentially so many more, depending on the asset class and the complexity of the deal you are negotiating.

For that property in Singapore, the biggest motivator for the vendor was speed of execution—getting the opportunity locked away and initial deposits paid over, and making sure the pricing integrity of the building was maintained. We knew that if we could meet that criterion, then a lot of other terms were movable. And move they did. In the end we secured a smaller discount on the purchase price but incredibly favourable settlement timelines and terms, which was actually the most important element for us, as the existing price was sharp already.

Sometimes price is not the most important element in a negotiation. Get to know the vendor's motivation for bringing a deal to the table to begin with, and structure your negotiation to give them as much as you can of what they want. Then ask for the terms you want and go to work to structure something that's a win–win for all parties involved. To me, this is the only way to do business.

Now your terms are locked down, you're ready to secure the deal.

Securing the deal

It's time to take the deal off the market, ensuring you have the appropriate clauses in the contract to protect you if you are still arranging finance and doing aspects of due diligence.

It's all about having all of your ducks in a row and being market ready. Up to this point you've had to be ready to move and move fast, as the deal is still on the market to other potential investors. If you're not ready to act decisively, you will simply miss out on the deal or you'll be expending time, effort and even money researching the deal when someone else has already snapped it up from under your nose. This is where having a clear strategy, a solid due diligence framework and a world-class wealth team on your side can make all the difference.

Managing emotions

Emotions can play a significant part in your investing journey, and if you're not aware of them and how they play out for you during this journey, it can turn out to be expensive.

Now you have your name on a contract, the pressure is on; for some people, that pressure can feel overwhelming and buyer's remorse kicks into gear. Out of fear, you pull the pin on the deal—for all the wrong reasons.

On the flip side, you may be overexcited because you have secured the deal. You have fallen in love with it, and in your eagerness you are overlooking warning signs or clear indications that there could be a problem. But instead of pausing the deal to examine them more thoroughly and perhaps renegotiate terms, or pull the pin altogether, you just charge ahead anyway because you're caught up in the excitement.

Emotions inevitably play a part in investing. Try to understand the emotions of the other party or even the market, whether fear or greed are in play, or the emotional state of the renter or home buyer whom you are targeting when property investing.

But never, and I mean *never*, make your investment decisions based on emotions. Successful investors make decisions based on strategy, facts and due diligence. The only space for considering emotions in investment selection is when assessing the emotional state of the market and who you might be dealing with on the other side of the deal.

Once you have ticked off all outstanding conditions, it's time to finalise the contract and move on to installing it in your portfolio.

Before we touch on this aspect, I want to mention the importance of relationships and trust here. Just as it's important to you that a deal provider has a reputation for being trustworthy and as good as their word, you must be too. When you are building a deal flow system and your own network, you have to look upstream at the relationships that extend well beyond the person who presented the opportunity to you. They have relationships they are managing upstream also, and it's critical you respect them. If you don't, then you are putting their relationships in jeopardy, which are potentially worth hundreds of thousands, if not millions, to them. I can tell you now that if you do that, they will never bring you another deal. You are simply too risky to deal with.

This doesn't mean going with every deal; it just means being a good person to do business with. Do that and keep watching the deal flow expand.

One of the reasons my wife and I were presented with that Singapore opportunity was simply because we have the relationships in place already and a reputation with the agent we were dealing with for acting decisively, even if the decision is a no for this particular opportunity. The deal was there; they needed someone to move fast, and because we could, it came to us first.

Step 4. Manage efficiently

A massive congrats to you! You've got the deal done, and now it's time to install it in your portfolio.

To manage your investment portfolio effectively after acquiring a new asset, it's essential to focus on organisation, monitoring and strategic adjustments. Here are some key ways to ensure this is done well, safely and efficiently:

Set your rhythms.
- weekly money night
- monthly check-in
- quarterly review.

Set your document management process.
- **Record details**. Document all relevant details about the new asset, including purchase price, acquisition costs, expected returns and any financing terms.
- **Maintain legal documents**. Store legal documents, contracts and agreements securely, either digitally or in a safe physical location.

Use tools to manage your portfolio.
- **Use portfolio management software**. Incorporate the new asset into your existing portfolio management software to track its performance alongside your other investments.
- **Automate data entry**. Set up automated data feeds or manual entry processes to keep track of performance metrics such as cashflow, appreciation and expenses.

Manage your portfolio performance.
- **Establish benchmarks**. Set specific performance benchmarks based on the asset type, market conditions and investment goals.
- **Schedule reviews**. Conduct regular performance reviews (monthly, quarterly) to assess whether the asset is meeting expectations.

Manage risk and diversification.
- **Review diversification strategy**. Ensure the new asset complements your existing portfolio and does not overexpose you to any one market or risk.
- **Implement stop-loss orders or hedging strategies**: For liquid assets, consider stop-loss orders or hedging strategies to minimise potential losses.

Manage and minimise tax obligations and ensure compliance.
- **Understand tax implications**. Be aware of any tax obligations or benefits associated with the new asset. This includes capital gains tax, property tax or other relevant taxes.
- **Ensure compliance**. Ensure all compliance requirements are met, especially for international investments or those with specific regulatory requirements.

Get cashflow clarity.
- **Track income and expenses**. Maintain detailed records of all income generated and expenses incurred by the new asset.
- **Set up reserves**. Establish a reserve fund for unexpected expenses or market downturns related to the new asset.

Rebalance portfolio as needed.

- **Evaluate asset allocation**. Assess the impact of the new asset on your overall portfolio allocation. Adjust if necessary to maintain your desired risk/return profile.
- **Rebalance regularly**. Regularly rebalance your portfolio to align with your investment strategy and market changes.

Leverage professional advice.

- **Consult financial advisers**. Work with financial advisers or portfolio managers to make informed decisions about the new asset's integration.
- **Engage with legal and tax experts**. Seek guidance from legal and tax professionals to ensure all aspects of the asset's management are compliant and optimised.

Implement security measures.

- **Data security**. Ensure all digital records and systems used for portfolio management are secure, with robust cybersecurity measures in place.
- **Backup records**: Regularly back up all important documents and data to prevent loss in case of technical failure or cyber-attacks.

Stay informed and educated.

- **Monitor market conditions**. Keep an eye on market trends and conditions that may affect the asset's performance.
- **Continue learning**. Stay updated on best practice in asset management, market analysis and investment strategies.

By implementing these strategies, you can manage your investment portfolio efficiently and safely, ensuring that new assets contribute positively to your overall investment goals.

You have now completed an entire deal flow cycle! You found the deal, did effective due diligence, executed efficiently, installed it, and are now free to get back out and start again—all the way back to doing your numbers and fine-tuning your strategy—after you have added your first or another investment to your portfolio on your continuous journey to taking back your freedom.

Got it? Good. Now get out there and do it again!

Power points

- Even the most well-crafted and strategic plan means squat if you don't find the deals that will make the difference in your portfolio.

- Average deals bring average results.

- The best deals are done off-market.

- The four parts to the deal flow system are:

    1. **Access opportunity.** How do you get access to off-market deals to begin with?

    2. **Assess viability.** How do you conduct rapid, top-level due diligence on a deal to get to a strong YES or a strong NO?

    3. **Execute rapidly.** Once you have a deal, how do you secure it and execute on it quickly and safely?

    4. **Manage efficiently.** Install the deal in your portfolio, freeing you up to go back and hunt for more.

- The four levels of due diligence are:

    1. **Macro.** Identify broad trends in the location, country or region, or even globally. These overarching trends typically impact everyone.

    2. **Micro.** Focus on specific, sector-focused and short-term factors that can impact investment decisions and market momentum.

    3. **Asset.** This due diligence dives into evaluating the specific asset itself.

4. **Analysis**. The final due diligence level focuses on the numbers, ensuring that all financials align.

- When you are building a deal flow system and your own network, you have to look upstream at the relationships that extend well beyond the person who presented the opportunity to you.

Meet Tony

I'm Tony, a 62-year-old small business owner who spent over 35 years working 60-hour weeks. For most of my life, I lived on autopilot, accumulating lessons and what I thought was moderate wealth. But when I turned 60, reality hit me—I realised my wealth hadn't grown much in 20 years and retirement felt like a distant pipe dream.

I'd always been interested in wealth-building, reading *Rich Dad Poor Dad* and attending seminars, but life kept getting in the way. I felt stuck, frustrated, and unsure how to change my financial trajectory.

One Saturday morning, while watching a property auction show, I saw Todd Polke in an interview. His conviction and sincerity captivated me. He spoke about wealth creation and planning in a way that resonated deeply. Though I hesitated at first—he looked young enough to be my son—I decided to email him. To my surprise, he responded the very next day, and we set up a time to chat.

It wasn't easy to follow through. Old habits and excuses crept in, but Todd didn't give up on me. He was direct, persistent, and invited me to attend one of his seminars. Stepping out of my comfort zone to attend was the best decision I ever made. That day marked the beginning of a complete transformation.

The Power of Guidance and Community

I quickly realised the impact of being surrounded by like-minded people with shared goals. The support and knowledge available are phenomenal. Todd's program pushed me to step out of my comfort zone, take charge of my financial future, and put in the effort to make it happen. His guidance, systems and opportunities helped me take control of my money and my life.

It has been challenging and exciting. The most dangerous thing is staying stuck in our comfort zones as we are trained to. Take the bull by the horns and make your money work for you—not the other way around. Anyone can do it; it's about making the right choice.

Transformative Milestones

Since working with Todd, my financial outlook and personal life have completely changed:

I sold underperforming properties, including a holiday home and rental properties, and reinvested in stronger opportunities which delivered real results.

Over four years, I purchased six properties. Recently, three of these properties have increased in value by over $500 000 each, adding over $1.5 million to my portfolio.

- I have multiple income streams flowing in from high income generating opportunities
- I have positioned myself for big potential future profits from strategic business investments
- My Bitcoin investments have grown by 600 per cent, significantly boosting my portfolio.
- I downsized my business operations and purchased a smaller commercial property to reduce overhead costs, reclaiming valuable time.

Through every step of this journey, Todd has been by my side, guiding me and opening doors to opportunities I would never have accessed on my own. As a layperson, these deals and investments would have been out of reach. Todd's consistent support and regular check-ins have ensured everything stays on track.

In just five years, my net worth has grown substantially, and by the end of 2023, I moved to Cairns to begin my retirement with my wonderful partner, Barb. With all units and developments completed, established income streams, and financial freedom secured, we purchased our dream home on two acres, complete with renovations and a pool.

Barb has joined me on this journey, and Todd has been an incredible support for us both. Together, we've built a shared vision for our future and continue to explore exciting opportunities.

This isn't just a financial plan—it's a lifelong journey. Todd has become more than a mentor; he's a trusted friend to both Barb and me, as well as his family.

If you have the chance to work with Todd, don't hesitate. Yes, it's hard work, but staying stuck on the hamster wheel of life is so much harder. You have to step out of your comfort zone and take control of your future.

The only way forward is to get off this merry go-round and make of your life what you want, we only get one shot here make the most of it. I wish I had started so much earlier but then I would not have had the fortune of meeting this amazing young man, Todd. It is never too late to start

Give it a go—you won't regret it. And remember you don't know what you don't know until you realise just how much there is to learn. Todd will open doors you never thought possible.

PART VI

BUILDING LASTING WEALTH

CHAPTER 16

CONSTRUCTING YOUR FINANCIAL FORTRESS

Living in the 21st century, we enjoy many privileges made possible by technological advances and improvements in our standard of living, and we take certain types of freedom for granted—but are we truly free?

In a world where a financial crisis can lead to mass job losses, where during a pandemic you can be forced into lockdown, unable to leave your home or run your business, where you can be tracked all over the internet, where there's more surveillance and more government financial control than ever before—and more coming—ask yourself, *how in control do you really feel?*

In reality there has been a systematic erosion of your liberties. Your choices, your privacy, even your control over your future are at risk. And it is up to you to put a stop to it and take back control and ownership of your finances and your future.

We think we are free, but we are still being manipulated and controlled by governments, tax offices and big corporations.

A kind of modern-day slavery does exist, but it is covert, hidden in plain sight. This is financial slavery, and if you are like most people it has been keeping you in invisible shackles, stopping you from truly living and experiencing the life you want. It keeps you chained to the middle.

It's time to free yourself.

Freedom isn't something that one day magically appears. It's something you must take back, piece by piece, one freedom at a time.

The four freedoms

There are four freedom milestones you will pass on your way to living your ideal life and creating your legacy, and each milestone you achieve opens an opportunity to accelerate your results.

- Emotional
- Location
- Time
- Financial

Emotional freedom

The first shackle that keeps you locked in place is the programming for living the default (middle) life. Taking back your emotional freedom means freeing yourself from the belief systems, programming and expectations of others and all the excuses we hold for ourselves about why not me, why not now?

We have invested a lot of time in this topic. If you have completed the money lens exercise you are already well on your way to doing some serious cleansing and rewiring. Time to free yourself once and for all from the middle-level mind traps you have inherited and created for yourself, and to look through a clean money lens and make your millionaire mode switch.

Location freedom

The second shackle to break is the job or business that confines you to a specific location, locking you into a fixed schedule reminiscent of the industrial age.

Location freedom is about reclaiming autonomy over both where and when you work. Instead of being required to show up at an office for eight hours a day, five days a week, you set your own schedule and choose your workspace. You may still trade time for income, but location freedom allows you to move away from the confines of clocking a set number of hours. If you finish your work in four hours, the rest of the day is yours to enjoy or build towards your future.

This freedom lets you be intentional with your time. As long as your tasks are completed, you can decide how to use the extra hours. Essentially, you can be anywhere on the planet whenever you wish. Whether it's lounging on a beach in Bali, sipping coffee in Paris or snorkelling off the Great Barrier Reef, anything's possible when you're not tied to one place.

In the 21st century, you have more geographic freedom than ever, thanks to affordable travel and universal internet. However, location freedom also requires financial resources to support travel and maintain your lifestyle while on the move. With the right balance, this freedom can reshape your life and work and take you a further step out of the middle pack who are all swimming along in the same direction.

Time freedom

The third shackle is our addiction to busyness and the feeling of being stuck on a treadmill. Achieving time freedom means decoupling your income from the hours you work. The outdated belief that more time equals more money isn't true; if it were, all employees working long days would have already achieved financial freedom. When your income is tied to time you become your own bottleneck, as everyone draws on the same resource of 24 hours in a day. This is one of the biggest anchors for most people stuck in the middle.

When you break this link, your income potential grows. Instead of exchanging time for money, you start exchanging value for money. This shift provides more freedom to choose how and with whom you spend your time.

So how do you reclaim your time freedom? By increasing your value and earning based on the results you create, not the hours you work.

Recently I had an electrical issue at home due to a cut underground cable. After going through three electricians without a permanent solution, I found Alex. He fixed the problem in 25 minutes. Later I received a high bill and initially questioned the cost, since he was there for less than half an hour. But then I asked myself some better questions: Did he provide the result I wanted? Yes. Did others fail to provide that outcome? Yes. Did he save me time and frustration, and ensure my family had electricity? Absolutely. Was I happy to pay for the value he added? Without a doubt. And I'd call him again in a heartbeat.

This illustrates a key distinction: the wealthy spend money to buy time, while the poor spend time to save money. Successful people understand that time is their most valuable resource, and they invest in buying it back whenever possible.

Financial freedom

The fourth shackle is lack of a real-world financial education and addiction to consumer debt and living by a set of money rules designed to keep you in the middle.

Financial freedom means the income to support your life is earned by assets you own and control. This is achieved by investing, whether in investment assets or in a systemised business that operates without you.

The income flows in whether or not you work. You have your most valuable asset—time—back under your control. Now it's time to move up the rungs of the Financial Freedom Pyramid, from *needs* to *wants* to *dreams* to building your *legacy*.

Decision-making control, location control, time control and financial control—each boils down to control and it's critical for you to regain mastery over each of them.

That control brings financial sovereignty, which is in essence what I teach investors how to do: to take back complete control over their financial decisions and future, free from reliance and influence of external factors, and never again to feel they are held to ransom by anyone or anything.

So how do we go about creating this? Remember the end goal of wealth building that we discussed earlier in the book: to build a sustainable, diversified portfolio of quality assets that deliver a consistent and reliable income stream into your bank account to fund the lifestyle you desire.

The key words there are *sustainable*, *consistent* and *reliable*. Building wealth will help you escape the middle; keeping your wealth will help you stay out and realise your freedom.

As someone who has had the experience of losing almost everything and having to start again, because I wasn't as vigilant in this matter as I should have been in the past, I can attest to its importance and am now hypersensitive around its effective implementation for investors.

Your financial fortress

Let's face it, everything won't always go just right. Your wealth building won't always follow a gentle upward trajectory. Challenges and dangers won't always gently tap you on the shoulder to alert you that they're coming. Sometimes they come fast and hit hard, and your future wealth depends on your ability to ride out the inevitable reverses that arise.

This is the longevity factor you need to be striving for. Without it, you can feel unprotected and vulnerable. But when you have invested in setting this up correctly it's like walking around with a suit of armour on designed just for you.

Figure 16.1 (overleaf) illustrates how to construct a *financial fortress* in your life.

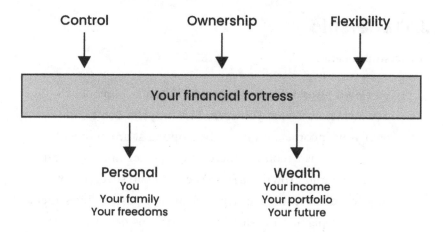

Figure 16.1: your financial fortress

There are three keys to a rock-solid financial fortress:

1. Control—the key to being in control of your future choices
2. Ownership—the key to staying safe and sovereign
3. Flexibility—the key to adapting to changing circumstances, markets and opportunities.

Let's review each of them.

1. Control

Control means...

- choices—in how you live your life free from external forces
- privacy and identity control—protecting your privacy and identity so you keep your business *your* business
- income and cashflow control—ensuring you control where and how your money flows, and who gets paid first
- sound body and mind—physical freedom and freedom from media influence.

2. Ownership

Ownership means...

- **you own your income streams.** You take control of how, when and what you earn. In a job, you don't truly own your income, and it can be stopped at any moment. Job security is becoming increasingly uncertain, especially with the rapid growth of AI. True financial sovereignty requires diverse income streams, such as passive investments (rental properties, dividends, interest), business ventures, side hustles and intellectual property. By managing your earnings, you reduce reliance on a single source that could vanish unexpectedly.

- **you own your assets.** Extending beyond just having assets in your name or through legal structures, it means ensuring that assets (properties, businesses, stocks) are appropriately protected, managed and leveraged to create additional value and income. This is where a specialist investment accountant and advisers can be worth their weight in gold.

- **you own your investments.** Beyond traditional investments, this encompasses directly managing your portfolio and making informed decisions, and not relying solely on advisers.

- **you own the essential skills and knowledge.** This is perhaps the most powerful type of ownership as it can never be taken away from you. Even if things go wrong, the asset of your financial IQ empowers you, because you know you can build it all over again.

- **you own the creation of your legacy.** Planning for the transfer of wealth to future generations or charitable causes is part of your financial sovereignty. It's about establishing a clear legacy plan, including estate planning, trusts, wills and family education on managing wealth responsibly.

- **you own your time.** Having control over how you allocate your time is crucial. It might involve building passive income streams that free up time, outsourcing tasks or setting up systems that allow you to focus on high-value activities, such as strategic planning or exploring new opportunities.

3. Flexibility

Flexibility means...

investment flexibility. Maintain an adaptable investment strategy that covers your overall approach, investment structures, asset allocation, asset classes and cashflow. This flexibility enables you to adjust to market changes, switch between defensive and aggressive tactics as needed, and stay consistently on course towards your ultimate financial freedom goals.

Here are some core principles to apply as a guide to approaching the construction of your financial fortress.

It's personal

There's no one-size-fits-all strategy. Some educators claim that a single structure suits everyone, but this overlooks the unique nature of each person's personality, business, situation, goals and values. While there may be common elements, your plan must be tailored to you.

> *Implementation:* Knowing the financial freedom figure, or FFF, end goals and lifestyle you want to create, what are some key elements of the financial fortress you want to install? *Who is in your fortress?* Describe the level of safety, security and privacy protection you want to provide.

Start early

Implement when the seas are calm. Don't wait until a storm has struck or is on the horizon to try to create a safe shelter. It won't be strong enough. It won't have proper planning, and ultimately you likely won't be protected.

> *Implementation:* Note the potential future risks you want to protect against.

Own nothing, control everything

An old maxim of the wealthy is to structure things so you control them, their movements and cashflow but own none of it so it cannot be taken away from you.

> *Implementation:* Note what feels unprotected and at risk in your situation right now that you would like to shore up.

Focus on the primary outcome

Remember why you're setting this up in the first place: for asset protection, right? You may have other agendas, such as reducing your tax, but these are secondary, and you don't want to sacrifice the integrity of your armour to reduce tax.

> *Implementation:* List in order your key outcomes in setting up your financial fortress, such as safety, privacy, legacy, tax reduction, asset protection, income protection and job security.

Not a substitute

Asset protection is just one part of building a financial fortress around you, your business and your family. Structures alone can't replace proper insurance, cash or equity buffers, and effective cashflow management to navigate financial challenges.

> *Implementation:* List other key action steps you need to take to help you navigate current or future potential financial challenges.

Regular review

Monitor and adjust continually. Building a financial fortress is not a set-and-forget process. Regularly review your financial structures, investments and protection strategies to ensure they remain effective and aligned with your goals. By actively monitoring your portfolio, you can make timely adjustments to optimise performance and security.

> *Implementation:* Schedule a financial fortress audit as part of the review rhythms you implemented from earlier chapters.

Plan for the unexpected

Sustainable wealth means being able to ride out the ups and downs of life. You do this by planning ahead for the inevitable what ifs. Ensure you are set up with sufficient buffers, insurances and protection mechanisms to give you security and choices when you need them most.

> *Implementation:* Create a contingency plan that outlines steps for responding to potential scenarios such as job loss, market downturns or health issues. This can include adjusting expenses, rebalancing investments, temporarily reallocating resources or maintaining wealth pockets in different parts of the world.

Get diversified

To construct a financial fortress and achieve financial sovereignty, your portfolio needs to be diversified across five key areas:

1. **Strategy.** Use a mix of asset types, including buy and hold, paycheque (income-generating) and momentum assets. This ensures that your portfolio covers all essential elements for balanced growth, income and capital turnover.
2. **Asset.** Diversify across various asset classes and sectors, such as real estate, stocks, bonds and commodities, to reduce the impact of market fluctuations.
3. **Geographical.** Spread investments across different locations and jurisdictions to avoid reliance on a single market, mitigating region-specific risks. This way, too, you will not have everything under the government's watchful eye.
4. **Time.** Incorporate short-term, medium-term and long-term assets to establish different liquidity points, allowing you to withdraw chunks of cash at various stages and reinvest based on new opportunities.
5. **Risk.** Diversify among different opportunity providers to avoid key person or market risks. Include a mix of stable growth assets, reliable income streams and higher-risk, high-reward plays to accelerate your portfolio's growth while managing risk.

Implementation: Outline your current portfolio diversity and what additional diversity you need to implement as part of your overarching wealth and freedom plan.

End in mind

Your asset protection isn't just about where you are and what you have right now; more importantly, it's about where you're going.

Set up your structures with what your future portfolio is going to look like, as once an asset is in a particular entity, it can be difficult and expensive to change it.

> *Implementation:* Review your current portfolio, if you have one, and consider your next potential investment. Ask: What kind of structure should I put this asset in? My personal name? Do I need to set up a trust or company or other entity? Who should I get this advice from and when?

Align with your core values — invest with purpose

Your financial fortress should reflect your personal values and long-term goals. Invest in assets and strategies that align with your beliefs and ethical considerations. This alignment creates a sense of purpose, ensuring that your financial journey supports your overall life vision and aspirations.

> *Implementation:* Write down what values-based investing means to you, and list what kind of opportunities you are happy to invest in and those that would be a no for you.

You now have the foundation for building a rock-solid financial fortress to protect yourself, your family and your portfolio. However, this doesn't have to be just a portfolio to help you realise your freedom. This level of portfolio can truly do some good.

If managed the right way, it's the type of portfolio that could last for generations. You can pass your knowledge down to your kids and teach them to do the same for theirs.

This could be a portfolio that makes a positive impact on the planet, leaving the world in a better place than you found it. This is about creating wealth that will outlast you. It's the beginning of a legacy.

Power points

- Your liberties—your choices, privacy and control over your future—are being eroded. It's up to you to reclaim control of your finances and your future.

- Freedom isn't something that one day magically appears. It's something you must take back, piece by piece, one freedom at a time.

- The four freedoms:

  1. Emotional freedom means freeing yourself from the belief systems, programming and expectations of others and all the excuses around why not me, why not now?

  2. Location freedom is about reclaiming autonomy over where and when you work.

  3. Time freedom means decoupling your income from the hours you work.

  4. Financial freedom means the income to support your life is earned by assets you own and control. This is achieved by investing, whether in investment assets or in a systemised business that operates without you.

- Instead of exchanging time for money, focus on exchanging value for money.

- The outdated belief that more time equals more money isn't true; if it were, all employees working long days would have already achieved financial freedom.

- The wealthy spend money to buy time, while the poor spend time to save money. Successful people understand that time is their most valuable resource, and they invest in buying it back whenever possible.

- The three keys to a rock-solid financial fortress:
  - control—the key to being in control of your future choices
  - ownership—the key to staying safe and sovereign
  - flexibility—the key to adapting to changing circumstances, markets and opportunities.
- There's no one-size-fits-all approach to investing. Strategies must be tailored to each person's unique personality, risk profile, financial situation, age, goals, values and knowledge.
- The five diversifications needed in a portfolio:
  1. **Strategy.** Buy and gold, paycheque and momentum ensures that your portfolio covers all essential elements for balanced growth, income and capital turnover.
  2. **Asset.** Diversify across various asset classes and sectors, such as real estate, stocks, bonds and commodities, to reduce the impact of market fluctuations.
  3. **Geographical.** Utilise different locations and jurisdictions to avoid reliance on a single market, mitigating region-specific risks.
  4. **Time.** Incorporate short-term, medium-term and long-term assets to establish different liquidity points, allowing you to withdraw chunks of cash at various stages and reinvest based on new opportunities.
  5. **Risk.** Diversify among different opportunity providers to avoid key person or market risks. Include a mix of stable growth assets, reliable income streams and higher-risk, high-reward plays to accelerate your portfolio's growth while managing risk.
- Your asset protection isn't just about your current position; it's about where you're headed. Build structures with your future portfolio in mind.

CHAPTER 17

CREATING LEGACY WEALTH

It was November of 2017 and I was deep in the world of cryptocurrencies and loving it, not just because of the profits I was making, but because of the philosophy behind it, the challenge it represents to the traditional systems, and its emphasis on decentralisation, privacy and trust.

But this is not a story about that.

It was about 1:00 in the morning and I woke up distraught and in tears. It took me a moment to gather myself together. I had this moment of realisation, somewhere in the space between unconsciousness and consciousness, that if something happened to me right now, my daughter would get none of the crypto wealth I had built because she wouldn't know where to go. I was the only one who knew what there was, where it was and how to access it. I was beside myself, because creating a legacy has always been of utmost importance to me, but it went deeper than that. If I was no longer around, how could I pass down the things I had learned about life and wealth and more?

I grabbed a pen and paper and started writing furiously. I spent the next three hours scratching out what became the first draft of my legacy plan, in which I laid out everything from what I owned and how to access it, and who to talk to get help and what my wishes were—the usual things. But money, I thought, wasn't the only legacy I wanted to build. I have so much more in me to pass down and prepare my daughter for.

What about all I had learned about life and money and wealth building? What about the life lessons? What about some of my network who could help guide her? I wanted to prepare her to be able to handle the wealth I was going to give her. I began setting out my wishes of the mentors she would work with, the people I wanted to support her, the training she would need to pursue, and the kind of wealth that should be generated when and why. She has to learn how to manage money before she is given it.

By 4 am I had finished. It was still deep night and I was exhausted but feeling relieved and thankful for the lesson. Before I went back to bed I sent my mother a message, as I figured I had better let someone know where to find this plan. The message simply said 'Hi Mum. If something happens to me, look here for some stuff for Annabelle,' and I pressed send.

Oops! She was on the phone straight away asking if I was okay and what was wrong and asking if I'm in trouble. I apologised profusely and explained that everything was fine and to go back to bed. My poor mother.

I had watched this movie called *The Ultimate Gift*, about a deceased billionaire, 'Red', who leaves his spoiled grandson Jason a series of tasks to perform (or 'gifts', as it were) leading to what he called the 'ultimate gift'. The movie follows the fundamental mind shifts within Jason as he completes each of the tasks his grandfather had set him. Red wanted his legacy to be more than an inheritance; he wanted to pass on important life lessons, which he hid in these tasks—lessons about work, money, friends, learning and more. Ultimately Jason emerged a different man in every way, but it wasn't just Jason who benefited from Red's 'gifts'. To me the film's message was profound, and it shifted my way of thinking and my understanding of legacy.

I believe it's not enough just to leave money or assets behind. I think we all have gifts far greater than that to give, and that's where our true wealth lies. That's the wealth that outlives you.

I have spoken on thousands of stages, and one question I often ask is, 'Who here wants to give back to the world in a bigger way than you are right now?' Almost every hand in the room goes up, every time. I believe there's a natural desire in all of us to contribute, even if we haven't yet figured out how. My view is that you should make as much money as possible, take care of your own life, then find a cause greater than yourself to give back to. Part of your life's mission is to discover what that is and pursue it wholeheartedly.

Legacy is about building wealth that spans generations. It's about passing down the lessons of a life well lived. Finding a cause bigger than yourself and leaving the world better than you found it. Discovering your purpose and using it to benefit others.

Your mission is to uncover your most valuable legacy and to give it fully.

The wealth you create is in direct proportion to the vision you hold. I want to invite you to elevate your level of thinking. Together, let's build part of your legacy vision right now.

Your legacy vision

There are four cornerstones to your legacy vision (see figure 17.1) that, when you are clear on them, can become a guiding light to how you plan your entire life from this day forward. Your sense of meaning expands, your decisions become more intentional, your mind is clearer and your wealth is more targeted.

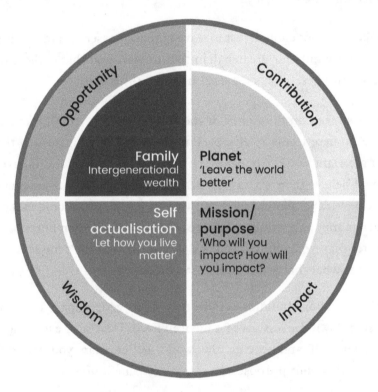

Figure 17.1: the four cornerstones of your legacy vision

Cornerstone 1: your mission/purpose—Who will you impact? How will you impact?

I believe we are all here for a reason. Each of us has a mission, and part of our journey is to discover it and live it to the fullest.

You were not born just to exist or drift through life. You were born to make an impact, no matter how big or small.

At core I'm a teacher. I empower investors to take control of their finances, grow their wealth and reclaim their freedom. But beyond financial strategies, my true mission is to help people rise above their struggles so they can explore their deeper purpose. I believe everyone has something valuable to give back to the world, and my goal is to ensure they have the time, money and capacity to pursue it fully and leave the world in a better place than when they arrived.

So what might your impact be?

I know this is a big question, and I don't expect you to have your mission and purpose fully figured out. If you do, fantastic! If not, these questions and processes will help you begin your journey of self-discovery.

In my mid twenties I spent years wrestling with the idea of finding my mission and purpose, then I realised that the journey itself is part of the discovery. By asking deeper questions, I tapped into new levels of awareness and growth. That realisation allowed me to take a deep breath and let go, understanding that my purpose would reveal itself when both the world and I were ready.

In the meantime I asked myself, *What is the closest path to what my purpose might be?* Then I took the first step. As I walked that path, new experiences and insights opened up. I grew, and I started to uncover more of what I was meant to do and who I was meant to become. I kept asking that question, over and over. And piece by piece it began to come together. But you know what? I'm still asking questions and diving deeper every day.

Here are some questions for you:

- What is your purpose? (If you can't describe it yet, what is the closest you can get to it at this time?)
- Who do you want to influence?
- How will you have that impact?

In leaving your legacy you want to ask yourself: Who do you want to impact and how do you want to have that impact?

Cornerstone 2: self-actualisation — a life well lived

What if we lived so fully that our very existence became our legacy? A life well lived means wisdom we can pass down to future generations. This was the legacy Red passed to Jason—the gift of experience and the wisdom it brings.

I often say that the greatest reward in building wealth and success is not in what we gain, but in who we become along the way. That's a legacy worth sharing—living a life of purpose and showing by example what it means to pursue life wholeheartedly.

So why not decide this in advance? Be intentional in the lessons you want to share. Be intentional in who you want to become. Be intentional in the legacy you build by being the fullest version of yourself.

Let me introduce you to my great-grandfather Sir John Beales Chandler (known as 'JB'). I never knew this man—he died well before I was born, when my mother was just seven. But through the stories passed down to me, I've come to know a man whose life continues to make an impact.

I first heard about how this 5-foot-3 young man with red hair came out to Australia at the age of 20 as a near-penniless immigrant and cut cane in Queensland. I learned how, although he was small in stature, he was big on hard work and courage.

My mother shared stories of the first general store he opened, which grew into a nationwide chain. I even remember visiting Chandlers electrical stores as a boy. I learned how he founded the radio station 4BC (for Beales Chandler or Brisbane City) in 1930; how he later acquired 4BH, built a media empire including a TV station, and served as chairman of the Chandler group of companies until his passing.

JB was a serial entrepreneur and a pioneer.

He served four consecutive terms as Lord Mayor of Brisbane, starting just before the Second World War, and founded the QLD People's Party, which later became the Queensland division of the Liberal Party. Known as the 'Little Man' who brought efficiency to the city council, he believed in giving back to society for the opportunities that had enabled his success as a businessman.

JB lived his life in service to others. During the war he opened up his home for the war effort, and during his terms as Lord Mayor he never wore his robes of office—he was too modest for that. In 12 years he never took the salary afforded the Lord Mayor and instead gave it back to the city. He was a generous and humble man who truly cared.

JB was knighted in 1951 and the Brisbane suburb of Chandler was named in his honour. He held positions on several boards and established multiple organisations within the broadcasting and electrical industries.

This man was a force to be reckoned with.

In 2021 I attended the Queensland Business Leaders Hall of Fame induction where Sir John was posthumously inducted. All my life I have heard stories about this man from my mother, who learned from her own parents the same lessons I'm passing down to my kids. To see him honoured in this way for the impact he had on industry and the community was an emotional moment I will truly never forget. His was truly a life well lived.

What does 'a life well lived' mean to you? How do you want to be remembered? Imagine you have lived your life in its fullest expression, what are three lessons you would choose to leave behind you?

I asked this question recently of a room full of investors, and here are some of their responses:

'I want my daughter to know who she is at her core, not to be swayed by what others say about her but to be strong in how she feels about herself.'

'It doesn't matter what life throws at you; it's about being able to enjoy it while it's happening. Sometimes, when we're under a lot of stress, we wait for the end rather than enjoying the journey.'

'I work in the international education and migration industry. What I learned during COVID was that when there are no international students coming in and the borders are closed, life can throw rocks at you. But use those rocks to build a castle, stay committed and move forward. After facing those difficulties, you gain a sense of resilience and realise you can get through anything. That's the biggest lesson I've learned.'

In leaving your legacy you want to ask yourself: How will your life become your greatest message to others?

Cornerstone 3: family — Intergenerational wealth

It has always been important to me to build wealth, not just for my children, but for future generations. To give them choices that otherwise they might never have. It takes just one person to shift an entire lineage.

Now, some might think, 'The little bastards can figure it out for themselves, I'm spending all my money', and fair enough if you want to do that. Others might want to lend a helping hand and still others to build a formal legacy.

As I write this, we are in the middle of an affordability crisis. The cost of living is soaring, and housing affordability worsens each year, not just in Australia but globally. Many people I speak with fear that their children may never be able to afford their own homes and worry they may face poverty. Personally, I think first home buyers will someday be museum exhibits, with property mostly passed down from one generation to the next.

The growing divide between rich and poor is increasingly evident. Like it or not, it's happening, and you must decide which side of that divide you want to be on. What choices do you want for yourself and your children? Will the legacy you create and pass on include assets, income streams, businesses or wealth systems that generate lasting cashflow?

Simply giving money away isn't enough; in fact, it's potentially irresponsible if detached from any accompanying understanding and values. It's up to you to teach your kids these things.

Personally, I don't want to raise spoilt brats, and I also don't want the hard work I have put in to be screwed up by stupid decisions, which could have been prevented by education and understanding. I have every intention of being that dead guy still controlling his wealth from the grave with a big smile on my face!

Here's a wealth cycle that has played out through generations:

- The first generation, deciding they want something more from life, creates the wealth.
- The second generation, having witnessed the hard work and learned the values of wealth building, grows it.

- The third generation, born into money, without the same appreciation, understandings or value systems, blows it.

I run a lot of virtual trainings with the investors who work with me and my team, and it makes me so happy when I see their kids being involved and coming along to live events. I love it.

Never be afraid to talk about money and investing with your kids. Get them involved. If you don't normalise wealth creation in their lives, by default they will fall into the societal norms smack bang in the middle.

When I think about intergenerational wealth, it's not just about passing down money. The real value lies in teaching your children—and their children—how to be responsible stewards of wealth, generous individuals, and people who want to have an impact on the planet—as givers, not takers.

Here are a few questions to get you started with your intergenerational wealth plan:

What financial or lifestyle opportunities do you want to be able to pass on to future generations?

What keeps you up at night when you think about your family's financial future?

How will you prepare your kids to become stewards of wealth and for them to prepare their kids in the same way?

In leaving your legacy you want to ask yourself: What is the wealth and what are the choices you want to create and leave for your family?

Cornerstone 4: planet — leaving the world a better place

How will the world be better because you were here?

I believe we all have a responsibility to give something back to the world that has given us so much. The question is, how will you choose to do that?

For many, the drive to contribute stems from personal experiences, and that's certainly true for me. Not many know that I was born in the Solomon Islands, a small string of islands off Australia's north-east coast. It was a unique upbringing, with some of my earliest memories being my parents walking off the beach to go scuba diving.

The moment I turned 12 I got my open-water diver's licence and immersed myself in the ocean's beauty. I have had the privilege of diving and experiencing some incredible sites. I have also encountered spots where I've watched plastic bag after plastic bag float past me and seen what were once beautiful coral reefs damaged or destroyed.

Conservation of the Oceans is one of my contribution projects.

My father has an enduring love for Africa—the adventure, the unspoilt nature and the incredible ecosystems. I have lost count of how many times he's been there. As I write this, he's in Africa again, chasing monkeys up a hill. One of my most memorable trips was trekking in Chizarira National Park in Zimbabwe. It was special because it was so close to my dad's heart, and he wanted to share it with us.

It was just my dad, my two brothers, a guide and a camp boy. We trekked every day, camping in beautiful spots, falling asleep to the sounds of lions and hyenas. One day, we stumbled upon the carcass of a bull elephant, its tusks removed. It was a horrifying sight. Since our guide was a ranger, we went in search of the poachers responsible. This experience ignited my passion for land conservation and wildlife protection.

For Nerissa, who is obsessed with animals, her dream and mission in life is to start animal foundations. She and I are both also passionate about conserving the Amazon, where we have both spent time. It is about preserving habitat so the ecosystem can continue to thrive. We have also supported girls in developing nations through school and contributed to building schools and libraries, aligning with my passion for education.

What are some of the experiences you have had in life that have triggered a desire to help protect and give back?

Here are some audience responses:

'*Food security for children*'

'*I've been a farmer for 40 years. And my policy with my kids is that every year they've got to plant at least 1000 trees on one of our farms.*'

'*Mental health of the teenagers and kids growing up in this world, and what's ahead of them*'

'*Help people with addictions*'

'*Our daughter got sick bad once and ended up in the children's hospital. You see all the kids in there ... So every Christmas we buy all the kids in the hospital gifts to give them something to smile about.*'

Here are a few questions to help shake out further ideas:

What breaks your heart about what is going on in the world right now?

What do you want to give back at a higher level than you are doing now?

How do you intend to give back? Is it money, time or expertise, for example?

Remember that none of this needs to be grandiose. It might be on a small scale, and that's perfect. You do what you can, with what you have, where you are.

> 'We do not inherit the Earth from our ancestors; we borrow it from our children.'
> — attributed to 19th century Native American leader Chief *Seattle*

Crafting a legacy wealth plan is not only about financial prosperity; it's about making a lasting impact. It's the lives you touch, the new choices you make possible, the values you instil and the positive change you generate. So seize the opportunity today to design a plan that not only secures your financial future but also shapes a legacy whose ripples will be felt for years and decades to come.

In leaving your legacy you want to ask yourself: How do you want the world to be better because you were here?

Power points

- I believe leaving behind just money or assets isn't enough. Our greater gift is the legacy that outlives us.

- Make as much money as possible, secure your own life, then give back to a cause greater than yourself.

- A legacy means not only creating wealth that endures for generations, but passing down lessons from a life well lived, supporting causes greater than yourself and leaving the world better than you found it. It's about discovering your purpose and using it to uplift others.

- The wealth you create is in direct proportion to the vision you hold.

- The four cornerstones of your legacy vision:

  1. Your mission/purpose—who will you impact and how will you impact them?

  2. Self-actualisation—the wisdom you pass down from a life well lived

  3. Family—creating intergenerational wealth

  4. Planet—leaving the world a better place.

- The true value is in teaching your children—and future generations—to be responsible stewards of wealth, generous individuals and people who aim to make a positive impact on the world as givers, not takers.

- Our greatest reward in building wealth and success is not in what we gain, but in who we become along the way.

- Giving money away without sharing the understanding and values to manage it is irresponsible.

- A legacy wealth plan goes beyond financial prosperity; it's about creating lasting impact. It's in the lives you touch, the choices you enable, the values you instil and the positive change you inspire.

CONCLUSION

I remember when I first began living beyond the middle. I hadn't yet built my wealth. I still had a job and bills to pay. I didn't have the freedoms I do now, but my mindset had shifted. It was as if I had stepped through the gates into a whole new world.

I remember all the opportunities that started flying at me. There were so many, and they were bigger than I had ever experienced before. I asked myself: Had these opportunities always been there but I was just unable to recognise them? Did I feel like I didn't deserve them? Was I just not ready to receive all of the abundance that life has to offer?

And I remember the people who showed up in my life. They were different. They talked about different things — about goals, dreams, success and possibility. Where had these conversations been before? Why had I not attracted them? Why was I not starting them myself?

I found I saw work and business through a different lens. It had taken on a new meaning. Never again would it be about exchanging time for money. Now it was a different game — about how much value I could add as well as how much wealth I could create.

Investing became a way of life. I knew then it wasn't reserved for a special breed of people; anyone could embrace it, no matter what their starting point. Investing was about so much more than buying some assets.

It became one of the core philosophies of my life—to invest in growing myself as a person, in skills to grow my earning ability, in relationships to expand my network and meet more interesting people, in opportunities, in mentors who could fast-track my results, and of course in the assets and income streams that meant my money was working hard for me even while I was sleeping.

And as my understanding expanded, my wealth and freedom inevitably expanded along with it. It felt like I had been a racehorse with blinders on, charging down a single lane, focused solely on reaching the finish line, wherever that finish line was. But now the blinders were off, and I could finally see so much more around me.

Beyond the middle a new world is waiting for you. It's a world that is open to anyone who has the courage to take this path. But the path is not without its challenges, that's for sure. Here are a few things you may experience that likely no one has warned you about.

You are going to let some people down. Starting out on a brand-new path, you're going to be breaking a lot of rules that other people take for granted around who you are and how you should behave. Your actions will challenge their version of reality and who you are supposed to be. They may question you, warn you, even ridicule you. They may say things like, 'Who do you think you are?', 'Stop trying so hard', 'It will never work' and 'Be realistic.'

Understand that what these people are really saying is, 'Please fit into my model of the world, of what is possible and what I feel comfortable with.' The truth is your drive and success will make some people uncomfortable, because it will force them to reassess their own lives, which can be painful if they are compelled to admit they are not living the life they were meant to.

So you will have to learn to be okay with disappointing people when you stop living according to their expectations and following their rules.

Be prepared for the internal battle. As you step into this new version of yourself, you will inevitably face the internal battle between the old you who doesn't want to change, who has been conditioned for years, if not decades, into a certain way of thinking, doing and being, and the new you who is just finding their feet in the world living beyond the middle. And you have to decide at any given point who is going to win.

Who will win when you are beset by self-doubt? Who will win when you find yourself falling into old habits and patterns of thinking? Who will win when the safety of the old you and the known feels so enticing when your path becomes unclear?

You need to sit with the discomfort for a time, until you fully embrace who you are becoming. You must be willing to say no to the mediocre in order to say yes to the exceptional.

Your people may change. Be prepared for shifts in your peer group as you embark on a new path. This has been my own experience and is one shared by many who choose to grow and evolve. You may find that the new you does not resonate with the people you used to spend time with—sometimes even close friends or family members. Conversations that once felt engaging may lose their appeal, while talking about the things you care about now make them feel uncomfortable. You may even catch yourself holding back parts of who you truly are in an effort to fit in. You sense that you're operating on a different wavelength, leading to a natural distancing.

This doesn't necessarily mean saying goodbye to these relationships entirely, though for some that may happen. You can invite them to grow alongside you or simply, lovingly, accept them as they are while choosing to spend more time with people who align with your new mindset and way of being.

Focus on *who* you are becoming. Wealth building is less about what you acquire and far more about who you become along the way. Material gains may come and go, and are certainly fun, but the person you evolve into is lasting. That growth is a gift, not just for you but for future generations, as it can be passed down as a legacy that reaches far beyond material wealth.

This journey empowers you to take control of your future as never before. Remember, *you* are your most valuable asset. By growing yourself, you expand your ability to create, sustain and enjoy the wealth needed to live the life you envision.

If there's something in your life you haven't yet achieved, ask yourself: *Who do I need to become to reach this level of success?* Then craft a plan to step into that next-level version of yourself and make it happen. Growth is the foundation of lasting wealth—and it all begins with you.

The journey to success is challenging by design; if it weren't, everyone would already have reached the finish line. That's why you need to make reaching your goals a non-negotiable commitment and to set wealth and financial freedom as the standard you refuse to compromise on. Then hold yourself accountable by being uncompromisingly tough on your excuses so they no longer stand in your way.

Remember, change and progress are not the same. Change is inevitable, but progress? That requires deliberate effort and intention.

At its core, *Escape the Middle* isn't a book about money, it's a book about freedom. And true freedom extends far beyond financial wealth. True freedom is spending every moment of your life doing what you love, with the people you cherish most. It's the ability to travel anywhere in the world without being tied down by a 9-to-5 job. It's the power to buy what you desire without worrying about the price tag. It's living each day to the fullest with purpose and intention.

True freedom means making bold, unconventional choices because you no longer need to conform to anyone else's expectations. It's found in the adventures you enjoy and the meaningful conversations you share. It's the freedom to give generously to the causes and communities you care about. Most important, it's the freedom to live life entirely on your terms—the way *you* want to.

This book is here to help you achieve what matters most—true freedom defined on your own terms. But remember, learning is only the first step; implementation is what truly creates change. That's why I've included plenty of free resources to help you take action. Visit www.escapethemiddle.com/resources to get started.

Take it one step at a time. As I tell all my investors, *learn one thing, do one thing.* And repeat after me: 'My life works to the level at which I keep my commitment.' Make that your new mantra. Commit to following through and escape the middle once and for all.

In reading this book you have already made an investment—of time and money and attention and brain space—and I deeply respect and salute you for doing so. You're setting off on a beautiful and deeply rewarding journey, and I'm honoured to have played a part in it.

Let me share something close to my heart: my true mission, which lies behind everything I do, is to empower good people like you, who want to make a bigger impact on the world, to reclaim your freedom, to rise above your financial struggles, to gather the resources you need to create meaningful change and to fully embrace your purpose on this planet.

I want you to achieve financial abundance, master your world and live an extraordinary life. I hope this book inspires and equips you to step out of middle and into extraordinary.